Get That Job!

The Quick and Complete Guide to a Winning Job Interview

Thea Kelley

Foreword by Orville Pierson

Author of *The Unwritten Rules of the Highly Effective Job Search*

Plovercrest Press

D0167540

Published by Plovercrest Press, Albany, California USA

Cover design by Vanessa Mendozzi Design
Book design by justyourtype.biz

ISBN 978-0-9983808-0-3

First Edition

Dedicated to you.

May you get a great job, sooner!

Contents

Foreword

I'm Orville Pierson, and I'm writing to tell you why I think
Thea Kelley's interviewing book should be included on a
job hunter's reading list. I also want to explain why I think
she may have broken some new ground in job search assistance. But before I do that, I want to give you some background on my experience and tell you a bit about career
services.

I've been doing job search assistance work of one kind
or another for about 40 years. I started with several smaller career transition companies. Then I spent 19 years as
Director of Program Design and Service Delivery at the
headquarters of Lee Hecht Harrison (LHH), a 300-office
global career services and outplacement company.

In that job, I led a team that created programs, books
and websites for LHH to use in assisting recently laid-off
job hunters in finding better new jobs more quickly. Our
main how-to-find-a-job book has now gone through several editions and has helped over a million and a half people
find good new jobs.

I also trained hundreds of career coaches, usually in
one- or two-day classroom trainings. These coaches were

not newbies. They were typically people with 10 or 20 years experience in the field. My role was teaching them how to use the new materials and processes created by my team. But there were always discussions where the coaches talked more generally about what works and what doesn't work in job hunting, so all in all, I think maybe I learned more than they did.

Over the years, LHH was often approached by people wanting to sell their job-hunting materials or websites to a large career services company. When that happened, I was the person who reviewed those offerings and reported to our financial team on their value for job hunters. Later, when I began working outside of LHH with students and the general public, I also reviewed books and websites available to the general public.

I saw everything: the good, the bad and the really, really bad. People with extensive experience in recruiting, HR and career coaching usually provided good advice. But there were also people with little or no job search assistance experience who thought they had clever new ideas. More often than not, those ideas were known by experienced career coaches not to work. The "really bad" category sometimes included advice that would do job hunters more harm than good: telling lies, for example, or trying to trick employers.

Based on what I'd learned over the years, I wrote three books for the general public, in addition to the dozens that I wrote or co-authored for career services companies. Now, as an independent consultant and speaker, I continue to see new books and websites on job hunting.

I recommend that job hunters looking to be more effective start with books rather than websites. I do that because

Internet job search information tends to be a fragmented — and sometimes disjointed — collection of short articles on job hunting. It's often written by a number of unconnected authors, with little or no bio attached, so you don't know who's advising you. It's more like a collection of tips than a thoughtful overall approach. So I prefer books as a starting point, with the use of websites later in a job search.

When I first started in career work, most job hunting books covered the full range of job hunting methods and skills – resume writing, interviewing, using recruiters, networking and the like – everything in one book. Now, in a more complex world, I don't think it can be done in one book. The last time I looked, Amazon.com was selling about 15,000 books on job hunting, written by all kinds of authors. Most of these are only on one aspect of job hunting, not the whole thing.

So with that for background, here's what I have to say about Thea Kelley's *Quick and Complete Guide to a Winning Interview*.

First and most important, she did her homework. In addition to her work experience in the career coaching field, she has taken courses and read up on job search assistance. I read her book from cover to cover, and the advice is sound. She gives good solid guidance. This book is an overview of the most important to-do's and pitfalls. It's especially useful for someone who hasn't interviewed in a while or someone nervous about job interviews.

Another thing I like about the book is its length. This is where I think she's maybe broken some new ground. Her book is shorter than the average job hunting book, but offers more consistent and in-depth advice than you'll usually find on the Internet. I think she may have found a "sweet spot" on length. A series of shorter books like this one would be more manageable for job hunters than a collection of full-length books.

And Thea's book is easy to read. It's written in a way that you can easily scan it, looking for the areas most important to you. So it's maybe more of an Internet style of writing. Reading the whole thing is not a chore.

I very much like her emphasis on "authentic and strategic." I think it's important to be honest and to be yourself in an interview. But you have to be smart, too. You usually have only an hour. You need to make strategic decisions about what to say and what not to say – thinking about what's most relevant to the person you're talking to, and what will help you take the next step toward employment with that particular employer. Thea provides some good strong guidance on this.

So I'm glad you have this book in your hands. May you learn some things that will hasten your move to a great new job. And may you succeed and thrive in that work for a good long time.

Orville Pierson

Author of:

The Unwritten Rules of the Highly Effective Job Search

Highly Effective Networking: Meet the Right People and Get a Great Job

Team Up! Find a Better Job Faster with a Job Search Work Team

How This Book Will Help You Get the Job

Success depends upon preparation.

– Confucius (and many other people)

Asked what we do best, few of us would say "doing a great job interview."

Yet *this is one of the most highly rewarded abilities in life.* Skillful interviewing can be the determining factor in how soon you start getting that new paycheck – and whether you land your dream job or have to settle for something less.

This book will help you master this crucial skill so that you get the job and the career you want.

Get the job by being well prepared *and* being yourself.

Some people go into interviews thinking "I'll just be myself," but they're winging it, so it isn't their *best self* that the interviewer sees and hears. Others prepare by the cookie-cutter approach, memorizing answers recommended by experts and coming across as stiff and insincere.

My approach is based on authenticity and strategy, the "yin and yang" that work together for a convincing interview. You'll be *authentic* – honest and natural – while being *strategic* in presenting what the employer needs to know about the value you can bring to their organization.

You'll learn how to authentically and strategically use *every* aspect of the interview – from the first handshake to the last question and answer – to *stand out and get the job.*

What are your challenges?

Most job seekers face difficulties in interviewing. This book will explore issues like these:

"I'm not comfortable with talking about myself and 'tooting my own horn.' "

"I haven't interviewed in a long time (or ever)."

"I have trouble with certain questions, like 'Tell me about yourself' and questions about weaknesses."

"I tend to ramble. I start talking and don't know when to stop."

"I get so nervous, sometimes I go blank and forget what question I'm answering."

"I have a negative issue in my work history and I don't know what to say about it."

"I can't think of a story or example when I need one."

"I don't know what I'm doing wrong – I'm just not getting offers."

This book will provide strategies to overcome obstacles like these, and more.

In **Section One – First Things First: Preparing Your Core Messages** – you'll build confidence and clarity by identifying your key selling points and learning how to proactively emphasize those throughout the interview. Your answers will become more relevant, compelling and convincing.

In **Section Two – Questions: Answering and Asking** – you'll gain strategies for handling any question that may come your way, plus specific tips on dozens of the most common questions. You'll also learn to ask insightful and well-targeted questions that help you assess the job and impress the interviewer.

In **Section Three – Nailing the Nonverbals** – you'll polish the unspoken aspects of your presentation, including body language and clothes, and learn techniques for eliminating nervousness and self-doubt. We'll also explore how to stand out through effective use of "interview extras" like portfolios and presentations.

In **Section Four – Know What to Expect** – you'll get familiar with 12 different types of interviews and how to succeed in all of them. We'll also clear up some misunderstandings about references to make sure you sail smoothly from the final interview into an offer.

Finally, in **Section Five – Happy Endings and Great Beginnings** – you'll learn to conclude the interview effectively and follow up strongly, reinforcing the positive brand you've built up through the interview. You'll also get prepared to juggle offers, negotiate for the pay and working conditions you want and ensure a smooth transition into your new job!

This book is quick to read. Preparing to be the winner of a competitive interview process, on the other hand, takes time. So start now.

An interview can happen anytime. If you've sent out a single resume, or simply have a strong profile on LinkedIn, you could be called for a phone screening any day now. Recruiters like to take a casual tone in these "conversations," but don't be lulled: it's an *interview*. Even in-person interviews can happen on very short notice.

Work your way through these five sections and you'll be well equipped to stand out from other applicants and get the offer. So let's get started and get you ready.

SECTION I

First Things First: Preparing Your Core Messages

CHAPTER 1

What Makes You Stand Out? Your REV Points

If you want to stand out, don't be different; be outstanding.

Meredith West

In most interview situations, you have competitors for the job – maybe two, maybe half a dozen. You won't get the job just by being qualified – you need to stand out, and you need to be remembered.

Completing this chapter will prepare you to do exactly that.

Some applicants have tried to be memorable by using gimmicks – singing their interview responses, or wearing a tuxedo to show that the meeting was "a very special occasion." This will, indeed make someone stand out – but as a person of poor judgment, not as the right person to hire.

Let's plan how you will stand out for the best possible reasons.

I'm going to ask you to look at how you stack up against your competition. That may sound a bit daunting, but if you set aside your fears and take it one step at a time, by the end of the chapter I think you'll find your confidence has increased.

Less Is More: The Importance of Focus

Interviewing is a process of educating the interviewer. Educators know that if you hit someone with a huge bunch of facts willy-nilly, they may not learn anything. People learn better when the presentation is organized around a few core concepts.

Interviewing is also like sales and marketing. People in this field know that you don't sell a car by running through every feature it has. You focus on just a few: it's hip, cheap and fits into the smallest parking spaces. Or it's rugged, good-looking and roomy. You're competing for customers' attention, so you grab it with something simple and easy to remember.

In sales, these are often called "key selling points."

In an interview, the "product" you're selling is you. If that sounds awful, let's remember that you're not selling your soul — just clearly communicating the skills, expertise and personal strengths that will make you valuable to an employer.

In fact, let's get away from sales terminology. I call these your "REV Points," because they work best if they're **Relevant, Exceptional and Verifiable (REV)**. I'll say more about that later in the chapter.

Listing Possible REV Points

Right now, take a few minutes and jot down the top 10 reasons why an employer should choose you over the competition. (Later I'll ask you to narrow it down to no more than five.)

To help think of these, ask yourself questions like these:

+ What qualifications or skills do I have that are hard to find?

+ What do I do better than most of my peers?

+ What would my co-workers and managers say if I asked them what makes me valuable?

+ What have they appreciated most about me?

+ Am I the best at something, or the first, or the only one?

+ Is there an important area in which I am exceptionally knowledgeable?

+ What part of my job am I most passionate about? Am I especially good at that?

+ Do I have an exceptional record of promotions or career growth?

+ What is my most impressive professional accomplishment of the past five years?

+ Do have more education, training or certifications than is usual?

+ Have I won awards or been formally recognized for superior work?

Narrowing It Down

Now, let's pick the three to five points on your list that will be most impressive and convincing to an employer – the ones that will really sell you. To do that, as I suggested above, they need to be very Relevant, Exceptional and Verifiable.

Here's what I mean by these terms.

Relevant: A relevant qualification is in demand by employers. Study several job postings for the type of job you want, and underline the important skills, qualifications and qualities the employer is looking for. Which seem to be the top priorities?

Think about the likely *pain points* of your target companies – the problems that are eating into their profits or making them look bad. Skills that can help solve these problems are powerfully relevant.

Exceptional: An exceptional quality or qualification is one that *stands out*. Probably all of your competitors have experience in multi-tasking. But can they all speak Mandarin with the company's Chinese clients?

Working with me on his REV Points, Roger said, "The number one reason they should hire me is my integrity." But it didn't make his final list of points to emphasize. Why not?

Yes, integrity is hugely important in life and in work. But it's something employers tend to assume or take for granted until proven otherwise. In most cases it won't make you stand out in an interview.

Other qualities often seen as common include: hard working, intelligent, a people person, a good communicator. If you are *truly exceptional* in one of these areas, you'll need to prove it.

Verifiable: By this I mean that the item is not just a claim or opinion. It's something you can prove or give evidence for.

Facts are naturally verifiable. Let's say you believe your graduate degree is a key selling point. No problem, this is a fact and it can be verified with a background check. Likewise, your work experience is a collection of facts that can be verified.

Skills can be tougher, especially soft skills like communication. Most job applicants claim to have excellent communication skills. By itself, this claim is so subjective – such a matter of opinion, really – that it's almost meaningless. *Until you give evidence for it.* Your evidence might be something like this:

- The skillfulness of your spoken and written communications with the interviewer. (Thus, you're demonstrating these skills rather than just claiming to have them.)

- A story about the time when you diplomatically sorted out a misunderstanding and kept a client from leaving.

- The fact that you were sought out to provide coaching or training to new hires – especially if you were the only member of the team asked to do that.

- The fact that you wrote documentation that reduced service calls 50%.

- The fact that you worked on the school newspaper or consistently got A's in your English classes (if you're a recent graduate).

- LinkedIn recommendations praising your communication skills.

Now your claim of exceptional communication skills has credibility!

You'll notice that we're using these terms – verify, prove, evidence – a bit loosely. We're not talking about proving your skills with legalistic or scientific precision. The point is to be able to back up your claims enough to make them reasonably convincing to the interviewer.

Examples: Three Interviewees and their REV Points

Linda Smith, Human Resources Manager

1. Broad, abundantly demonstrated expertise in Employee Relations, Labor Relations, Compensation and Benefits, HR Information Systems and Analytics

2. Talent for strategic thinking (with stories to prove it)

3. Several awards for creating successful programs and initiatives

4. Inspires a loyal and high-performing team (proven by stories, LinkedIn recommendations and team members' career advancement)

5. MBA

Rick Johnson, Energy Efficiency Engineer

1. Five years experience in energy efficiency engineering

2. Experience conducting ASHRAE level 1, 2 and 3 energy audits leading to an average of 20% energy savings per building

3. Relevant advanced degree

4. Member of Technical Advisory Committee drafting Cordoba County's first Green Building Ordinances

Denise Williams, Sales Manager

1. Track record of consistently over-achieving goals and earning awards in Fortune 500 companies

2. Exceptional talent for effectively anticipating and navigating change through cross-functional collaboration (with stories to demonstrate this)

3. Learns quickly and positively impacts the bottom line within the first few months on any job (stories)

Which of your top 10 points really REV? Pick the top three to five and prioritize those in the order of how Relevant, Exceptional and Verifiable they are.

Together, these points make up your REV Agenda: the messages you will make a point of communicating throughout your interviews.

Now start memorizing these points. Put this list in a place where you'll see it every day. Look at it often. Do whatever you have to do to get it etched into your mind.

Congratulations! You have just built an extremely powerful tool that will help you not only in your interviews but throughout your job search, by focusing the minds of potential employers on a short, easy to grasp, easy to remember list of what makes you stand out as the person to hire.

Will Your REV Points Be the Same for Every Job?

No, your REV Points may vary as you apply to different jobs. For example, Sheila was applying to various jobs in nonprofit development (fundraising). When she applied at health-related organizations her MA in Public Health became a key selling point. At animal welfare organizations, her years of volunteering in her local animal shelter became more relevant.

However, if you're finding that all of your selling points are completely different from one interview to another, it may be that you're spreading yourself too thin in your job search. You may want to focus on identifying what you really do best, and proactively going after that.

How Will You Use These REV Points?

- ✦ **Emphasize them** throughout the interview process. These points go a long way toward creating your brand or unique identity in the employer's mind.

- ✦ **Know them by heart.** It's hard to build your communications around these points if you're constantly having to go searching for the list.

- ✦ **Take responsibility for educating your interviewer on these points.** If you meet an unskilled interviewer – for example one who asks the wrong questions, or one who talks the whole time and never listens – watch for opportunities to get your message across.

- ✦ **Start the interview with them.** People tend to remember what came first. A recent poll showed that 50% of employers believe they know within the first five minutes of an interview whether a candidate is a good fit. Focus those first minutes on what's important by making these points the basis of your answer to the first question in the interview, which is often "Tell me about yourself."

+ **End the interview with them.** People tend to remember what they hear first, but also what they hear last. Include some or all of these points in your closing statement at the end of the interview, as well as your follow-up communications.

+ **Develop stories (examples) from your work to bring each of these key points to life in your interviews.** (In brief bullet form, these stories can also greatly improve your resume and LinkedIn profile.)

Speaking of stories, you've probably heard that these are important in interviewing, and that you'll need a lot of them. How many do you need? How can you remember them when you need them? How can you make sure you'll tell them in a way that's clear, concise and memorable?

The next chapter will answer these questions, while helping you build an impressive, confidence-boosting tool kit of stories that *vividly demonstrate why you're the right person for the job.*

CHAPTER 2

Harnessing the Power of Stories

We learn best ... from hearing stories.

— John Kotter

What if you had a technique that would physically activate an interviewer's brain to make them pay more attention to you, grasp what you're saying more clearly, believe it more easily, and keep you at top of mind longer?

There is such a technique: storytelling.

Ordinary business communication – "I have extensive skills in yada yada yada" – engages only a small fraction of the brain, the parts that process language and logic. Stories do much more, activating multiple brain regions that work together to create multisensory, three-dimensional images and feelings. It's not just a description but an *experience*, so it's more convincing and more memorable.

Stories are a powerful way to communicate your skills in an interview, including those REV Points you developed in Chapter 1.

A Familiar Story?

I wonder if you identify with parts of this story.

Dan's "Broken Phone" – and How It Finally Rang
In four months of job search, Dan had completed a total of 11 interviews that went nowhere. He joked, bitterly, that his phone must be broken. It certainly wasn't ringing with offers.

Dan was a talented professional. He knew he could *do* the job. He just didn't know how to *talk* about his abilities.

Having read that he should tell stories, he had thought of a few, but not enough to get through a long interview. And when he told stories he would trip over his words, rambling on too long, uncertain where to stop and ending awkwardly. The interviewer would frown slightly, make a note, and move on to the next question in a neutral, uninterested tone.

And Dan wouldn't hear back. Maybe this sounds like the story of your life recently.

But the story's not over.

The Interview Success Project
One day, Dan said to himself. "Enough! I'm going to learn how to do this right."

He decided to approach interviewing the same way he would handle any challenging project that could earn him a great promotion: He would do some research, follow best practices and do the necessary work to ensure success.

Realizing that he might need 10 stories or more for each interview, and that employers in his field were requiring multiple interviews, Dan set a goal of developing 20-30 good stories that would illustrate his skills and demonstrate his value to employers.

Setting aside a few hours one weekend, he followed the instructions in this chapter and was able to build a list of 25 stories. He identified interview questions that his stories could answer, practiced telling his stories, and got feedback from others on how the stories worked.

His next interview sparkled with anecdotes as he painted a vivid, convincing picture of his outstanding work. The interviewer's eyes lit up with interest and the time flew.

In the end, Dan's phone rang with offers – from two companies, and he was able to choose the job he wanted most.

This chapter will guide you to overcome the difficulties that initially held Dan back and to transform your interviews and their results.

You will learn:

- How to gather and develop stories that prove your REV Points, those key reasons why you're the right person for the job.

- How to have enough stories – more than you think you can – so that you don't run out even if you go through multiple interviews at the same company.

- How to tell your stories clearly and concisely.

- How to remember the right story at the right moment.

SOAR: Anatomy of an Effective Story

A good interview story tells about a challenge you faced, the actions you took to solve it, and the results you achieved.

You may have seen acronyms like CAR (Challenge, Action, Results), PAR (Problem, Actions, Results) and SOAR (Situation, Obstacles, Actions, Results). Each of these acronyms provides a framework or model for telling a story. They're all good. ("Challenge," "Problem" and "Situation" all mean pretty much the same thing.) I'm going to use SOAR. So let's look at the parts of a SOAR story.

Example: Rob's Story *"Implementing SuccessSuite"*

Situation: "At the Cooper Company I realized our business management software wasn't helping us work efficiently."

Actions: "I researched the options, selected SuccessSuite, learned it, helped configure it and trained our staff on it."

Obstacle(s): "Management initially said SuccessSuite was too expensive. I prepared a presentation that changed their minds."

Results: "Efficiency was increased by 40%."

You may have noticed that this particular story has Actions before Obstacles, as if it was an "S-A-O-R" story instead of "S-O-A-R." That's okay, because the parts don't have to go in any particular order, although it's important to describe the Situation early in the story in order to set the scene.

The first thing you can learn from SOAR is *how very*

concise a story can be. If Rob needs to tell his story in 15 seconds, he can do it (possibly leaving out the Obstacle for brevity). That will come in handy, as you'll see later. On the other hand, he can easily expand into more detail.

Your Stories List

Start a new document in your computer called Stories List. Save it someplace you can easily find it, because you'll be referring to it often.

For each story in your list, I suggest you fill in the following:

<u>Title:</u>
Situation:
Obstacles:
Actions:
Results:

Let's get started. **Think of any work accomplishment you are proud of.** It may be a problem you solved, a process you improved, or a time when you went above and beyond your normal duties to get a job done. Now give that story a specific, unique title, like "Resolving Production Backlog last May" or "Filling In for Terry." Write that down in your list.

Then jot down a few words about the Situation, any Obstacles that arose, the Actions you took, and the Results. **There's no need to write full sentences or go into detail – you already know the story, and you won't be turning this assignment in!**

Once you've filled it all in, go ahead and tell the story

out loud (of course leaving out the title, which is just for your own reference).

Thinking about how you told your story, what worked well? What didn't?

Making SOAR Stories Work

Let's look at some tips for succeeding with each part of your story.

Situation

+ **Put the story in context.** Saying which job it happened at may be all the context you need. You may want to mention the year, particularly if it's recent, because employers especially value recent accomplishments.

+ **Identify the pain points.** If the situation was causing wasted time, lost money or missed opportunities, make that clear (without casting blame on yourself or others in your company).

+ **Keep it brief.** You're just setting the scene for the next three parts, which are more important.

Obstacles

+ **Obstacles are optional – they're a "plus."** You can have a perfectly good story that goes straight from Actions to Results. However, sometimes there was a big obstacle – an economic downturn, a microscopic budget, an aggressive deadline – that you overcame, making the story all the more impressive.

+ **Focus on the skillful way you overcame the obstacle or led others to do so.** If the obstacle was overcome through sheer luck or someone else's efforts, why mention it?

+ **Be tactful** if others in your company created the obstacles!

Actions

+ **Give just enough detail but don't get too granular.** If you're not sure how much to say, err on the short side, jump ahead to the Results, then ask the interviewer if they'd like to know more.

+ **Watch out for "we."** The employer isn't considering hiring your team, just you. That doesn't mean you mean you can *never* say "we," just make it clear what part you played.

Results, Results, Results!

+ **Don't skimp on describing the impact you achieved and how it benefited the company.** Companies hire for results, so be specific and complete about this piece.

+ **Quantify.** If you saved time or money, specify how much, even if you have to guesstimate. If you improved something, by what percentage?

+ **If you really can't quantify in numbers, use words.** Did you improve morale just a little, or significantly? Substantially? Dramatically?

+ **Give evidence that your work was great.** Did you earn a bonus or an accolade? Did your new idea become the standard operating procedure? Are they still using it three years later?

◆ **Give a sound bite.** Did your boss, a client or co-worker say something memorable about your accomplishment, either aloud, or in an email, or in a performance review? Quote it!

Again, the S-O-A-R parts don't have to be told in that order. For example, a brief mention of the results can be a dramatic way to start: *"Let me tell you about how I doubled market share in two months."*

And throughout your story, remember that you're telling the story in order to sell yourself as the best person for the job. Don't waste time on details that aren't relevant to that purpose.

Connecting Your Stories to the Interviewer's Questions

Of course, interviewers aren't going to say "Tell me a story." They're going to say *"Tell me about a time when you had to work with a difficult person,"* or *"Tell me about your experience with Excel tables / taking the lead on a project / team building / negotiation"* (or whatever is relevant to the job).

How can you help ensure that the right story will pop into your head? By keeping in mind what each story demonstrates, such as team building or negotiation skills.

For example, Rob's story, "Implementing SuccessSuite," demonstrates his skills in evaluating, selecting and configuring software, training, problem-solving, workflow analysis, process improvement, innovation, initiative, learning quickly, documentation development, troubleshooting, cross-functional collaboration and so on.

By noting these skills and strengths in his stories list,

Rob increases the likelihood that he'll think of this story when asked a question like "Can you tell me about a time you collaborated cross-functionally to solve a problem?"

Now go back to your own story list. Under your first story, list all the skills and strengths the story demonstrates. These are likely to include technical skills, "soft" skills like relationship-building and time management, specialized knowledge such as understanding best practices, rules or regulations, personal strengths such as dedication or initiative, and so on.

So now your list will look like this:

Title:
Situation:
Obstacles:
Actions:
Results:
What this story demonstrates (skills and strengths):

Stories are multi-purpose because most stories demonstrate multiple skills. So don't skimp in identifying the skills and strengths each of your stories demonstrates. Writing them down will help you connect your stories to the interviewer's questions.

Tip: Create question-and-story flashcards.

Get a bunch of 3x5 cards (or you can create digital flashcards in Evernote). On one side of each, write a common behavioral interview question like "Tell me about a time you identified a possible problem and took action to prevent it." (You can find lots of these questions by searching online.)

On the reverse, write the titles of two or three of your stories that could be used to answer that question. (One story isn't enough; you might have already used it during the interview to answer another question, so you need alternates.)

To practice with the cards, flip through the deck looking at each question to see if you can remember the stories that go with it. Just start with memorizing which stories go with which questions. Then, for more in-depth practice, you can actually practice answering the questions.

More Stories, Please!

How many stories do you need? Lots!

It's not uncommon these days to have multiple interviews for one job, involving multiple behavioral interview questions in each interview. Plus it's a good idea to tell stories for some of your non-behavioral questions as well. And it's best not to repeat the same stories in all of those multiple interviews, since the interviewers may compare notes afterwards. You don't want them thinking you have only a few noteworthy accomplishments.

Shoot for 20 stories or more. Does that sound impossible? Here's how you can come up with more SOARs than you think you can:

- **Look to your key selling points (REV Points).** Do stories come to mind illustrating these? Such stories might be some of your most important ones.

- **Practice answering behavioral interview questions.** Go through dozens of them. Don't get stuck on any question you can't answer — move on to the next one. You won't have an answer for every question, but whenever you do, immediately add that story to your list.

- **Use job postings.** Find job announcements typical of your job goal. For each bit of experience or skill mentioned, ask yourself: "When have I done or demonstrated that successfully?" Add any stories to your list.

- **Harvest stories from your resume, LinkedIn profile, performance evaluations and any kudos you've received.** All of these sources may contain, or spark your memory of, useful stories.

Once you do this, congratulate yourself on having created an awesome job interview tool that will help you get your next job, not to mention boosting your confidence and providing new material for your resume!

The 15-second Story

Often it's appropriate to take up to a minute to tell a story in an interview; or even two minutes.

At other times you'll need make it *very short*. For example, if asked "Tell me your three greatest strengths," you should illustrate your answer with an example or two (or even three), while still keeping the whole answer down to a minute or less. So any examples would need to be very short, perhaps 15 seconds.

A 15-second story can also be very convincing as part of your answer to "Tell me about yourself." I'll say more about that in the next chapter.

Theoretically, any story can be told in as short a form as necessary. Here's *The Lord of the Rings* in 15 seconds: An evil magic ring that threatened all of Middle Earth turned up in a small country town. A diverse team of comrades combined their skills to carry the ring through many dangers – including a vastly powerful enemy who wanted it for his own evil purposes – to Mount Doom, where it was destroyed, saving the world.

The key here is just to move through the SOAR steps with as little detail as possible. Here's that same story broken into SOAR components:

Situation: An evil magic ring that threatened all of Middle Earth turned up in a small country town and had to be destroyed.

Obstacles: Many dangers got in the way, including a vastly powerful enemy who wanted it for his own evil purposes.

Action: A diverse team of comrades combined their skills to carry the ring to Mount Doom.

Results: It was destroyed, saving the world.

Try it with one of your own stories. Cut the story down until you can say it in 15 seconds, or 20, or 10. Time yourself. (Really do that!) You're learning to be concise, a crucially important interviewing skill.

One of your first chances to use a very-briefly told story will come in the very first interview question: "Would you please tell me a little bit about yourself?"

If you're like most interviewees, your reaction to that first question ranges from puzzlement to outright dread. What to say? Where to start?

The next chapter may transform this into your *favorite* question, one that builds your confidence, makes you look good and gets the whole interview off on the right footing – on *your* agenda.

CHAPTER 3

Acing the #1 Interview Question: "Tell me about yourself"

You only get one chance to make a first impression.

– Will Rogers

The first handshakes are over and everyone is seated. "So," begins the interviewer, "tell me about yourself."

I call this the #1 interview question, for two reasons – because it typically comes first, and also because it may well be the most important. Your answer is a crucial first impression: the first time they've listened to you talk. Like the first eye contact, it's a defining moment. (So in a way, you do get more than one chance to make a "first" impression.)

If you're like most job seekers, you dread this question (technically, more of a command). Who can blame you? It's so vague. What on earth does the interviewer want to know?

A better question would be, what do *you* want them to know?

This question is a *carte blanche* invitation, an opportunity to focus the interviewer's attention exactly where you want it, on the reasons they should hire you – in other words, the **REV Points (key selling points that are Relevant, Exceptional and Verifiable)** that we discussed in Chapter 1.

Your answer to this question is your **REV Intro.** Let's look at how to prepare this powerful tool that will get your interview off to a very persuasive start – leaving you feeling more confident for the rest of the meeting.

Less Is More

Many candidates think they need to be complete in their answer, as if the employer had asked "Tell me *all* about yourself." Free yourself of that burden right now. You have the whole interview ahead of you. Details can come later.

Your REV Intro will be a brief, mile-high overview of what you bring to the table and what's special about you. *It's an introduction, not a book!* Keep it down to a minute or two.

No Matter How They Say It

There are various versions of the opening question. They might say "Can you introduce us to your qualifications?" or "How about walking me through your background?" or even a blunt "What's your story?"

No matter how they ask this question, what they're really saying is: "*Why should we hire you (instead of one of our other qualified candidates)?"* What do you have that the other candidates don't?

Craft an Answer That Sells

A REV Intro is based on those three to five REV Points you developed in Chapter 1. You can turn your REV points into a very effective "Tell me about yourself" answer by basically listing them. It's almost as simple as that.

Examples: REV Intro
You may recall Denise Williams, the Sales Manager in Chapter 1, and her key selling points:

1. Track record of consistently over-achieving goals and earning awards in Fortune 500 companies

2. Exceptional talent for effectively anticipating and navigating change through cross-functional collaboration

3. Learns quickly and delivers results fast

(These points have REV – they're Relevant, Exceptional and Verifiable. Points 2 and 3 sound like opinions but Denise will "verify" them by stories she tells later in the interview.)

So her answer to "Tell me about yourself" – her **REV Intro** – sounds like this:

"(Interviewer's name), based on your job announcement and my phone screening with (recruiter's name), it's clear the new person in this role needs to hit the ground running

and deliver results fast. That's what I've been able to do at Top Tier Technology; I transformed team morale and doubled revenues within three months. At Strong Solutions I achieved similar early wins, which my manager later mentioned in a recommendation on LinkedIn.

"As a manager, and earlier as a rep, I've consistently been well over goal, as you may have noticed from the awards in my resume. There are some interesting stories behind those, which I would be happy to tell if you like.

"Another need that was mentioned in the announcement – and something that's a specialty and a passion of mine – is to anticipate and capitalize on change. At Strong I saw how the new wearable technologies were creating opportunities for us, and I worked with Marketing and Product to maximize those.

"Would you like to hear more about anything I've said so far?"

For another example, let's look at Linda Smith, the Human Resources Manager. Linda's REV Points were:

1. Broad, abundantly demonstrated expertise in Employee Relations, Labor Relations, Compensation and Benefits, HR Information Systems and Analytics

2. Talent for strategic thinking

3. Several awards for creating successful programs and initiatives

4. Inspires a loyal and high-performing team (proven by stories, LinkedIn recommendations and team members' career advancement)

5. MBA

Those points became this **REV Intro:**

"I was excited to see that you're looking for someone with expertise in so many different areas within HR, because that's exactly what my background is like. I've been very fortunate that my 14-year career at Niagara, Inc. and Davis Direct has allowed me to gain experience in all of them – Employee Relations, Labor Relations, Compensation and Benefits, HR Information Systems and Analytics. I've managed all of these areas, and solved complex strategic issues in every one of them.

"For example... (two-sentence success story illustrating her strategic skills) ... for which I was recognized with a Top Performer award, one of four I've won during my time with EFG Inc.

"I couldn't have achieved any of that without a really engaged team. I'm very passionate about building that engagement. I get to know my staff individually and what their own goals are, then help them see the alignment be-tween those goals and department's needs. It has worked well; in the past five years I've had four team members promoted. I was sorry to lose some of them, but at the same time it was a great feeling seeing them reach their dreams.

"I'm also passionate about serving the business. My

MBA has helped me partner closely with leaders in various departments.

"How does that match up to what you're looking for?"

Essentials of a Good Answer

The examples above work because they have the following elements:

+ A focus on REV Points.
+ Just a little career summary.
+ Humanity – a bit of insight into personality or motivations.
+ Brevity – Denise's answer takes less than a minute and Linda's takes a minute and a half.
+ A natural, conversational tone.

The "Talking Points Outline"
(A tool for being prepared while still sounding natural.)

Planning your answer word-for-word and memorizing it – in other words, reciting from a script – does *not* make a good impression.

Scripted answers…

…don't sound natural, because people don't speak the way they write.

…are less believable, as if they're not your own words.

…may make the employer think you lack good

communication skills or the ability to think on your feet.

...are boring to listen to.

Instead of a script, create a bare-bones outline of your "talking points" to practice with, so that *the ideas are planned, but the words are fresh every time.*

Example: REV Intro "Talking Points" Outline

To illustrate what I mean, let's take the example of Rick Johnson, the Energy Efficiency Engineer from Chapter 1. Here again are his REV Points:

1. Five years experience in energy efficiency engineering

2. Experience conducting ASHRAE level 1, 2 and 3 energy audits leading to an average of 20% energy savings per building

3. Relevant advanced degree

4. Member of Technical Advisory Committee drafting Cordoba County's first Green Building Ordinances

Rick planned a REV Intro that basically lists his key selling points, adds some reasons he is attracted to the job he's interviewing for, and finishes with a question that forms a smooth hand-off back to the interviewer.

His outline may not make much sense to you or me, because he wrote it for himself. All you need to understand from it is how brief you can be, and how you can use bullets, sub-bullets, symbols and abbreviations to create an extremely skimmable, memorizable outline.

REV Intro Outline

+ "For the past five years..."

+ >50 ASHRAE audits

+ 20% energy savings per building

+ ordinances

+ attracted to job because:

  + unique energy challenges

  + opportunities

  + born here & want to move back

  + after Master's, 1st job in IA

  + family in NV

  + backpacking

+ "What questions or comments do you have about anything I've said so far?" (Smile.)

This outline didn't tell Rick exactly what to say. It just reminded him what to talk about. That allowed him to practice answering in a natural, conversational manner. Soon he had the outline memorized – but the answer itself was given in slightly different words every time, so it always sounded fresh. And of course, he made minor tweaks to fit the different opportunities he interviewed for until he landed his new job.

Here's how his **REV Intro** sounded:

"For the past five years I've been an energy efficiency engineer with Adams Associates in Des Moines, working on residential, commercial and public buildings, so I have more than the two to three years you're asking for. I've conducted

more than 50 ASHRAE 1, 2 and 3 energy audits that have led to an average of 20% energy savings per building.

"I also lead a team that consults to public agencies, and I recently served as a member of a Technical Advisory Committee that drafted Cordoba County's first Green Building Ordinances.

"I'm very attracted to this job with the State of Nevada because of the unique energy challenges in this state and the great opportunities in this organization. Also, I was born here and I want to move back. After I completed my Master's in Mechanical Engineering Iowa State, it was natural to get my first job there, but I have family in Reno so it feels like home. Plus, I love outdoor activities like backpacking, and the area is so great for that.

"What questions or comments do you have about anything I've said so far?"

10 Steps to Your Great REV Intro

Now you can create your own outline, practice with it and be ready to ace the #1 interview question with your own strategic, natural-sounding REV Intro.

Get out the prioritized list of REV Points you developed in Chapter 1. Then follow these steps:

1. **Get your answer off to a good start.** Often the best way to start is by combining one of your top REV points with a one- to three-sentence summary of your career.

(Think it's not possible to sum up your career in a

sentence? Sure it is. How's this for a short career summary: "Dwight D. Eisenhower rose through the military to become a general and finally the 34th President of the United States.")

Denise, Linda and Rick also did this in the examples above. So can you.

Mention the number of years of experience you have *only if* that number matches or moderately exceeds what the employer is looking for.

2. **Move on to another REV Point.** Ask yourself: Which of my other points follows naturally after that? Segue into it. (Linda's answer is a great example of use of transitions: brief connecting statements that smoothly change the subject from one REV Point to the next. But don't get hung up on this; a transition can be as simple as saying "Also…"). Continue until you have included all of your REV Points.

3. **Include an example or two to illustrate your claims.** Put the "V" in Verifiable! But you don't need to prove every claim in this answer; it's more like a spot check. Giving one or two examples implies that you can back up your claims in general.

4. **Reveal yourself, without "TMI" (Too Much Information)!** Somewhere in your REV Intro – probably toward the end – add a little insight into who you are: talk about what motivates or inspires you, discuss your philosophy about your job, or even

share a personal interest if it supports your brand. Avoid irrelevant personal information such as your age.

It's usually best not to talk about being a parent, unless life experience with children's needs and interests is highly relevant to the job. You don't want the interviewer picturing you getting personal phone calls from the kids, leaving early, and so on (whether that really describes you or not). Keep children and work separate, starting with the interview.

Humor is a plus, as long as it's *absolutely* inoffensive.

Of course, avoid anything controversial – politics, religion and so on.

5. **Plan a good ending.** Otherwise, you may find yourself trailing off with something like "So yeah, that's about it." Clunk!

One great way to end is with an open-ended question (i.e., one that can't be answered with a "yes" or "no") delivered with a welcoming smile. This helps the interview develop into a conversation, a dialogue rather than an interrogation. And wouldn't it be useful to know the interviewer's reaction to what you just said? If you're lucky you might get some useful information here, and at the very least you've shown an interest in the interviewer's thoughts.

Advanced technique: A bolder and more memorable ending would be to ask a question that turns the conversation toward the employer's pain points – their most pressing needs – and how you can help meet them. *"So that's a little about me. May I ask a question?*

How do you plan to respond to the challenge created by (industry trend about which you have strong expertise to offer)?" This approach can work especially well if you understand the business well and have a knack for consulting or consultative sales.

OK, now you've got your rough draft. How do you work with this?

6. **Type it up in a neat, outline form.** Use bullets and sub-bullets to help organize your thinking. Use abbreviations and symbols to make it concise and visual. The more you make it easy to read, the less it will intrude on the process of expressing yourself in a natural way.

    There may be just a few spots where you want to memorize exact words. Put those words in quotes as Rick did, above. (Do this very minimally. Don't turn yourself into a recording!)

7. **Speak your REV Intro out loud, using the outline as your road map, and time yourself.** Your intro should be no longer than one to two minutes. If it's longer, prune it down. Remember, this is just the start of the interview. Whatever you delete can be said *later,* as the interview progresses.

8. **Adjust the outline as many times as you need to.** This is an iterative process, like "lather, rinse, repeat." Hone your outline patiently and it will guide you to success.

9. **Now, practice without looking at the outline.** (It may be helpful to memorize the outline. That's another reason for making the outline very concise and clear: it will be easier to memorize.) Did you forget something in one spot? Practice that spot, including whatever comes just before and after it. Continue until you can say the whole answer without looking at the outline.

10. **Get feedback.** Do some of your practice with a mirror, or better yet, take a selfie-video of your answer to see and hear how you're doing. Practice with a buddy or a coach and ask for feedback on what worked well and what could be better.

Together with your REV Points and SOAR stories, with your REV Intro you've now completed what you need to prepare for a winning interview. You'll find the remaining chapters easier now that you have these three fundamental pieces in hand.

I know, "practice, practice, practice" – it's easier said than done. How do you motivate yourself to practice? How can you practice in the right way so you're rewarded with substantial improvement?

CHAPTER 4

A Word about Practicing

An hour of practice is worth five hours of foot-dragging.
— Pancho Segura

Like any skill, interviewing improves with practice. You've probably thought about the difference between working hard and working smart. Here are some tips for *practicing smart*.

Make it painless.

What do you need to do to enjoy practicing your interview skills – or at least, not hate it? Start with a brief period of time for a practice session, like 30 minutes. Set a timer. When the timer rings, you're done! Easy peasy, huh?

Associate practicing with enjoyment by rewarding yourself with a treat when you're done. It can be as simple as a little snack, a cup of tea or a few minutes of doing something you enjoy. I enjoy petting my cat.

Focus on what you want rather than what you *don't* want.

For example, if you tend to say "um" or "uh" too much, start focusing on pausing silently instead. (By the way, you can relax about the occasional "um." Even the best professional speakers say it occasionally.)

Have a vivid vision of success.

Make a list of the specific behaviors you want to see in your interviewing, such as pausing briefly to consider the question that has been asked, moving through the key points of your answer, smiling and so on. Take the time to imagine yourself doing the interview that way – what it will look like, sound like, feel like – and getting a positive response from the interviewer.

Practice purposefully, not mindlessly.

Remember when you were a child and you were great at pretending? Use that ability now to *imagine you're really talking to an interviewer* – one who likes what they're seeing and hearing. Role-play with the same alert, friendly tone of voice and body language you want to display in the interview.

Do multiple sessions, not marathons.

Several short practice sessions will do a better job of imprinting new skills in your memory than the one marathon followed by a week of ignoring the whole thing.

If your practice isn't working, try it a different way.

If one of my recommendations doesn't work for you, figure out something else. Have you ever practiced a sport, a musical instrument, a craft? What has that taught you about practicing? Bring that wisdom to interviewing practice.

Enlist friends, web resources and/or a skilled interview coach.

Mock interviews with a friend or spouse are a useful supplement to practicing alone. Ask for honest feedback on what's working and what could be better.

Interview practice apps and websites can be helpful as well, ranging from general apps like Job Interview Question-Answer to technical interview practice sites like Pramp.

For the most customized and in-depth assistance, consider working with a professional interview coach. Interview coaches can be found on LinkedIn, Yelp or through a general Internet search; and of course, see About the Author for information about my own services.

Now that you've got ideas about how to practice, let's get back to the bread and butter of interviewing: answering questions. You'll come up with authentic and strategically smart answers to tricky questions like "Why did you leave your job?", "What are your strengths and weaknesses?" and dozens more.

In fact, we'll start with tips for dealing with *any* question at all.

SECTION II

Questions: Answering and Asking

CHAPTER 5

How to Answer Any Interview Question

Wise men speak because they have something to say;
fools because they have to say something.

– Plato

Answer Authentically *and* Strategically

Authenticity and strategy could almost be called the "yin and yang" of good interviewing – except that they aren't opposites. The opposite of authenticity is phoniness, and the opposite of strategy is randomness, or carelessness.

Many job candidates fail to be strategic. They may interview in an honest and straightforward way, but without being clear what messages they're trying to communicate or how their answers are going to get them the job (or not).

Being strategic means asking yourself "How is this question an opportunity to sell my abilities? Keep your eyes on the prize! This will make your answers more compelling and relevant.

Even "negative" sounding questions like "What is your weakness?" are an opportunity to sell yourself by showing that you are self-aware, realistic about your limitations and always striving to improve.

Being strategic means proactively taking responsibility for making sure your message comes across. Let's say you've got some great stories prepared, but nothing the interviewer says gives you an opportunity to bring them up. Make your own opportunity. Say something like "Speaking of X, may I tell you about …?" or "(Name), we haven't talked about X, but there's something important I wanted to say about that, if we have a moment…"

Being strategic also includes planning out answers to some of the more crucial or tricky questions you may be asked.

Other candidates don't come across as being authentic. They give "right" answers that reflect what they think the interviewer wants to hear, but the answers sound "canned" and insincere. Maybe they found these "right" answers in a book. Or they thought up their own answers, but they've memorized them, word for word, like a speech. This kind of presentation doesn't build trust, nor does it demonstrate good communication skills. And it's boring!

In mock interviews I often hear candidates struggling to give a perfect answer that has very little connection to what's true for them. I ask them, "Okay, forget about the interview version for now. Just between you and me, what's the plain answer?"

You might think of this as your "best-friend answer"

– one with no caution or polish, just the blunt truth. Usually this spontaneous answer, or at least part of it, contains *the core* of a perfectly good *interview answer*. It will probably need some pruning and polishing, but in the end, you'll be more authentic and believable than if you had gone straight for the safe and perfect, by-the-book answer.

No discussion of authenticity is complete without a word about lying. As we all know, people sometimes lie about their qualifications. In the short run it may get them the job, but it may result in termination if the lie is discovered – and quite possibly, far-reaching damage to their reputations. Even if the lie is never discovered, they live in fear and must hide their secret from everyone they work with. This is not necessary. There's invariably a better way to address tricky issues such as a long career gap, having been fired, a negative work incident or even a criminal record. (Some of these will be covered in Chapter 7, Common But Not Easy.)

Be both authentic *and* strategic in your interviewing and *let the interviewer see the best of who you really are.*

Know What the Interviewer Is Looking for

There are three unspoken questions an interviewer has about you, which you can think of as the **Three C's of Interviewing.** (The following is derived from a model developed by the outplacement firm Lee Hecht Harrison.) The three C's are Competence, Compatibility with the company culture, and Chemistry.

*Competence***:** Of course, the interviewer wants to make

sure you can do the job, and do it well. This is what we all tend to think the whole interview is about: whether the candidate has the necessary experience, technical skills and soft skills. But actually there's more.

Compatibility with the company culture: They also want to make sure you'll work well *in this particular environment,* especially if it's quite different from the organizations you've worked in before. For example, some organizations are very hard-driving and competitive, while others are more collaborative; some are very hierarchical and formal, while others are more open and want everyone to be a leader. Show the employer that you understand and appreciate their company culture and will work well within it. If you have more experience with that type of culture than your resume indicates, clarify that.

Chemistry: Last but not least, they want a sense that you'll "click" with the boss and team members and that they'll enjoy spending a big chunk of their waking hours with you, day after day. Don't underestimate or forget the importance of liking and being liked by the people you're meeting – *all of them,* including the receptionist, shuttle driver and so on. Much of this comes down to everyday things like friendly chitchat, showing an interest in people, active listening, and body language such as a firm handshake, eye contact and a warm smile. *In many cases, chemistry is even more important than competence.*

Understand Before You Answer

We've all been taught in school to answer quickly, but answering instantly in an interview can give the impression that you're not taking the question seriously, or that you have your answers memorized.

Answering too quickly can also lead to the embarrassing experience of realizing, in the middle of your answer, that you've forgotten the question. So pause for a moment – usually two to five seconds is about right – and repeat the question silently to yourself. If the question is long or complex, repeat it aloud to ensure you've got it right.

While you're at it, make sure you fully *understand* the question. Is it a behavioral question, requiring you to tell a story? Make sure you tell one. Does the question have multiple parts? Get ready to answer them all.

Is the question vague or unclear? Ask for clarification if necessary. "I'd love to answer that, and before I do, could you just clarify for me which aspect of..." This is skillful communication – and it will enable you to give a more relevant answer.

There's another major advantage in asking questions related to what's being discussed: it makes the interview feel more like a dialogue or conversation, and less like an interrogation. That makes it more enjoyable – and a person who enjoyed their conversation with you is more likely to want to work with you.

Listen Between the Lines

Think about what the employer is trying to find out with each question. Usually it's straightforward, as in "Tell me about your experience with (technique or task)." On the other hand, a question about your boss is indirect: it's really a question about *you*, and whether you're easy to manage, and whether you speak respectfully of others even when they're not present.

Be Specific and Concrete

Question: "What's your management style?" Answer: "I'm fair, my door is always open, and I coach my team to excel and help them move up."

This answer sounds trite, uninteresting and vague. It neither informs nor persuades! Why not? Because it lacks the specific details that would make it real and convincing. What do you mean by "fair"? Can you give an example? Do you have a special philosophy or motto about coaching? Can you tell a story about a team member whose career you helped transform?

Use Sound Bites

Public figures use sound bites – short, memorable phrases and slogans – because they are easily remembered when more wordy, generic language has been forgotten. Of course, you can't always speak in sound bites – it would be difficult and just plain weird – but as you think about your answers, watch for the kinds of short, expressive language that we all come across every day.

One candidate told me her motto at work is "Have fun, but get it done!" That's a memorable phrase. Another told me he created a bit of software that caused a teammate in a staff meeting to say "That's the coolest thing I've ever seen!"

It's not Shakespeare, but it packs a punch. Look for "sound bites" like these in your LinkedIn recommendations and performance reviews. Memorize them – they are quotes, after all – and sprinkle them into your interviews.

Keep It Positive

Never volunteer a negative about yourself, such as confessing to a weakness when the interviewer hasn't asked about your weaknesses.

Don't say what you didn't like about any past job, unless asked to do so.

Don't badmouth your former boss, co-workers or company. This is one of the surest ways to destroy your chances at a job interview.

Occasionally, a story about your own accomplishments might unavoidably mention challenges created by others: a co-worker not pulling their own weight, or an underperforming employee you managed. Be very tactful, respectful, objective and brief about the behavior. Preserve this person's reputation by omitting any information that would allow anyone to identify them.

Handle Negatives Skillfully

Sometimes you have to address a negative, as when you're asked a question about your weaknesses, mistakes and failures, or why you left (or were fired from) past jobs. These questions can actually be opportunities to demonstrate strengths such as transparency, resilience, and learning valuable lessons from experience.

To handle these type of questions effectively, follow these pointers:

- **Plan and practice your answers.** Planning your talking points is always smart, and these questions may even justify an exception to my warning about scripting exact language. And do practice with someone – a peer or an interview coach.

- **Use the "sandwich" technique: surround the negatives with positives.** "Why did I leave Positive Promotions? I loved my work there, and I played a key role in many major wins, such as (maybe three ultra-brief examples), which I can tell you more about today. Then I was diagnosed with Ravel Syndrome, and I had to take a year off to recover my health. Last month my doctor said I'm fully recovered and should be fine from now on. I feel great and I've been attending conferences and reading a lot to refresh my skills while looking for the right opportunity. I'm very excited about this opening."

- **Keep the negative part brief.** See the example above, where the reason for leaving the job takes up only one-fifth of the answer. It can be hard to be brief about something you have strong feelings about. Questions like "Tell me about a difficult person you had to work with" or "Why do you want to leave your job?" present a strong temptation to kvetch and commiserate, particularly when your interviewer has the natural empathy we often see among human resources folks. Resist that urge firmly.

+ **Set your feelings aside and speak in an emotionally neutral manner.** This may require that you work through those feelings ahead of time. Try journaling, talking to a trusted friend, reading self-help books or getting professional help. As every pro athlete or performer knows, state of mind is crucial to success.

+ **Don't create negative sound bites.** As author Jeff Haden has written, "Interviewers will only remember a few sound bites, especially negative ones. Don't say, 'I've never been in charge of training.' Say, 'I did not fill that specific role, but I have trained dozens of new hires and created several training guides.'" Rather than saying "I haven't" or "I can't," tell them what you *have* done and *can* do.

Know that the Interviewer Wants You to Succeed

Good news! The interviewer would like nothing better than to be wowed by you, to know that his problem – lacking an employee – is about to be solved. Begin thinking of the interviewer as a future colleague who thinks highly of your skills, and with whom you'll soon have a friendly and productive working relationship.

Be Concise

Long-winded, wandering answers can be a deal-breaker. Employers don't want to hire people who ramble on and don't get to the point, or who don't leave enough air space for others to talk – especially themselves!

How long should your answers be? Telling a complex

and important story, such as "the accomplishment you're most proud of," may warrant two minutes, or even a bit more. But most interview questions can – and should – be answered in less than a minute.

Does answering in less than 60 seconds sound difficult? Have you found yourself rambling in past interviews, unsure when or how to finish your answer? The next chapter will help you make a great impression keeping all of your answers *concise and to the point.*

CHAPTER 6

How to Speak Concisely

*If it takes a lot of words to say what you have in mind,
give it more thought.*

– Author Dennis Roth

*"Begin at the beginning," the King said, very gravely,
"and go on till you come to the end: then stop."*

– Lewis Carroll's *Alice in Wonderland*

One of the most common ways to fail a job interview is to give long, wandering answers to the interviewer's questions. You need them to be excited about you – not overwhelmed or bored.

Most interview questions can and should be answered in less than a minute. Others, especially where you're telling a story, may take two minutes or more. An answer longer than five minutes is probably a mistake.

Be concise. You've heard that before, but it's not as easy as it sounds. *How* can you do it?

Know What You Need to Say

The main cause of rambling is a lack of clarity about where you're going in your answer. In Chapter 1 you saw that identifying the Situation, Actions, Obstacles and Results in your SOAR story can help you cover the key points efficiently, like checking items off a list. And in Chapter 3 you saw how a talking-points outline can help you prepare a clear and concise answer to "Tell me about yourself."

Other common questions can be treated in the same way. Plan your answers by noting your talking points, then timing yourself as you use them to run through your answer aloud. After going through this process multiple times over a period of days, you're likely to find yourself being more concise even on answers you *haven't* prepared!

Know How to End

Sometimes we ramble because we're looking for an ending – something to tie up your answer neatly, like "...and they all lived happily ever after," or "...and that's how they saved the world." Interview answers can actually end in a similar way!

Here are **four ways to end your statements:**

1. **Results.** If you're telling a story you can end with the impact and benefits of your work: *"This new program increased revenues 20% and became the model for similar efforts in five other divisions."*

2. **Referring back to the interviewer's question.** *"So that's how I'd describe my management style."*

3. **Relating what you've said to the job/company you're interviewing for.** *"Have you had similar situations here?"* or *"Does that sound like a strategy that could work here?"*

4. **A question:** *"Is there anything more you'd like to know about what I've just said?"*

As you prepare answers, make a point of practicing each of these four types of endings, so that you get in the habit of using them.

Still "Going Long"?

Here are **two practice techniques** that are bound to make a difference.

+ **Give too-concise answers** (yes! actually *too* short!), followed by a question like: *"Would you like more detail in any area of that?"*

Once you've practiced lots of too-short answers, you can then make your way back towards a perfect "Goldilocks Zone" where your answers are not too short, not too long, but just right.

+ **"Bottom line" your answers.** In other words, when you find you're rambling, interrupt yourself with one of these phrases:

- "To get straight to the bottom line…"
- "And the essence of this story is…"
- "To make a long story short…"

…And then get straight to the point.

By now you're probably itching to get your hands on some specific interview questions. In the next chapter we'll look at many of the most common questions, with tips for answering them in a way that shows you at your best.

CHAPTER 7

Common But Not Easy: Questions You'll Need to Answer

*First learn the meaning of what you say,
and then speak.*

– Epictetus

*The trouble with talking too fast is you may
say something you haven't thought of yet.*

– Ann Landers

We all know many jobs are being replaced by automation these days; even by robots. But if you're interviewing for a job, it means the employer doesn't want a robot. Interviewers are sick of robotic, "canned" answers candidates have read in books. So instead of feeding you readymade answers, I'm going to help you think through and prepare your own answers – ones that are both authentic and strategic.

"Tell me about yourself."

This question is so important it has a chapter all to itself. If you haven't already read and worked with Chapter 3, now is the time.

"What is your greatest strength?"

Think about those key selling points you identified in Chapter 1. What's at the top of that list? It should be a strength that has all the REV factors: one that is Relevant, Exceptional and Verifiable. Illustrate your point with a story.

"Why should we hire you?"

Focus on your key selling points and how they relate to the organization and its needs. This may be very similar to your answer to "Tell me about yourself," but say it a different way, using different examples.

"Tell me about the accomplishment you are most proud of."

If you've done your work with Chapter 2, you have plenty of SOAR stories to choose from in answering this question. Your answer may be taken as a reflection not only of your skills but also what makes you proud – in other words, what you find valuable and motivating. Make sure your choice is highly relevant to the job you're interviewing for.

"Why do you want this job?"

What is it about the role, the product, the mission and/or the organization that excites you? List these things in your mind. Your answer should be built upon the items that are central to doing the job, the things that will motivate you on a day-to-day basis, especially that the role is a good fit for your interests and skills, and that you love the product or believe in the mission. You can also add, as a secondary reason, that you feel like you'll be compatible with the company culture or that you've heard it's a great place to work. Avoid emphasizing that you're excited about the money, the location or the hours.

"What's your ideal work environment?"

First, ask yourself why the interviewer is asking this question. Are they planning to go out of their way to make sure you have the ideal work environment? No? So why are they asking?

Once you think about it, you undoubtedly realize that they're trying to find out (a) whether their environment is similar to what you're looking for, and (b) whether you're reasonable and flexible in your expectations.

Focus your answer on common, reasonable factors that will motivate you to do your best – like a team environment, open sharing of information, or a focus on customer satisfaction. Don't talk about preferences that are more self-focused such as amenities or benefits, or superficial items such as the appearance of the office. And make it clear that you do not *require* ideal circumstances and can perform excellently under a wide range of conditions.

"Where do you see yourself in five years?"

Why are they asking you this?

For one thing, they want to know whether the job aligns with your goals, and thus whether you'll stick around. They may also be hoping you have some ambition. Ambitious people often make better employees. They're more motivated, and they may work harder and smarter. They make a point of growing their abilities.

On the other hand, those who come in with their eye on a higher position and view the current role only as a stepping stone may be impatient and lack commitment to the tasks at hand.

So give an answer that combines a desire to grow, on the one hand, with realism, patience and commitment on the other.

Before the interview, see if you can find information about paths to advancement from within the position. If the only position you can advance to is that of the person you're interviewing with, proceed with care! He probably won't like the idea that you have your eye on his job, so just talk about growing and taking on more responsibility.

In most cases you won't have much information, in which case it's safest to start with a general answer followed by a question, like this:

"Over the next few years I see myself building my skills, taking on more responsibility and moving up, if it's appropriate. Can you tell me about how others have advanced from this role?"

Note: Although the question often includes the phrase "five years," you don't have to be that precise in your answer.

More open-ended terms like "over the next several years" may be best.

"Why do you want to leave your current job?"

Some reasons are easy to talk about:

+ You like your current job, and are only interviewing because you saw another opportunity too exciting to resist.

+ You are successful in your current job but wish to make a career change that your current company can't offer you – e.g., a shift into a different industry.

+ There is no path for advancement from your current role.

+ You need to relocate to a different city or state, and your current company can't transfer you.

It's trickier if you're leaving because of a problem – that the company is poorly managed, your boss is difficult, or such.

It's ironic that while the number one reason most people quit jobs is because of their bosses, that is the last reason you can safely talk about in an interview. Likewise, it's poor practice to criticize your current company, especially if you would be revealing issues that are not publicly known.

As with "Why did you leave your past job," take a look at *all* the reasons you might want to leave, and focus on reasons that present you in a good light.

"Why did you leave your job?"

If you left and immediately started a new job, this is easy: you left for a better opportunity (or what you *thought* was a better opportunity, if it didn't work out).

But leaving without a new job lined up is generally a red flag, so this question is tricky.

The key is this: although one reason may dominate in your mind – probably the most emotional one, such as a personality conflict or issue with the boss – usually there are more reasons. List them all on a piece of paper. Then see which of these reasons makes the best impression.

Example:

Joe quit his job for the following reasons: (1) his boss was a micromanager, (2) the company, a hospital, had toxic office politics, (3) the circumstances made it difficult or impossible to move up into a better department, (4) he couldn't stay until he found a new job because the job left him no time or energy for job search, and (5) he also had an itch to move into the pharmaceutical industry.

Reasons 1 and 2 are a minefield that would be hard to discuss without presenting himself as a complainer who badmouths his former employer. But he doesn't need to go there; he can build a truthful answer out of reasons 3-5:

"While Bayworth Hospital is a great institution in terms of patient care, and I had three excellent years there, with strong accomplishments like the ones we've discussed, there really wasn't a path upward for me there any more (reason #3). It was time to leave and pursue my longtime interest in pharmaceutical companies (#5) like this one. The job was intensely demanding and it didn't leave me the energy to conduct a search. (#4) So I gave notice, helped the department make a smooth transition, and then left to devote myself to a full-time process of transitioning into doing what I'm most passionate about."

Why does this answer work? Because it's true, tactful, brief (30 seconds) and focused on the positive. It's also a great example of the "sandwich technique": surrounding a negative (the fact that he left) with positives (his respect for the hospital in certain ways, his accomplishments and his passion for the current opportunity).

What if Joe had been fired?

In a past chapter I said "Never volunteer a negative." Joe doesn't need to say he was fired, unless specifically asked (see the next question). His answer could be the same as above, with a slightly different ending:

"...It was time to leave and pursue my longtime interest in pharmaceutical companies like this one. Since then I've devoted myself to a full-time process of transitioning into doing what I'm most passionate about."

Because this subject is emotionally charged for Joe, he would be wise to rehearse this answer with great care.

Joe also needs to be prepared for the likelihood the interviewer will ask additional questions that will reveal that he was fired.

"Have you been fired? What happened?"

First of all, realize that having been fired is probably more of a big deal to you than it is to the prospective employer.

Keep your answer short and sweet: brief and emotionally neutral.

Here are some effective ways people have explained being fired:

+ I was a valued member of the team, as I've described, for five years. Then a new manager came in (or there was a reorganization, or the company was bought) and a large percentage of the staff and leadership were let go, including me. The new manager then filled the team with people he had worked with at a past company. The silver lining is that now I'm able to interview for this exciting new opportunity.

+ Looking back, I've realized the job and I weren't really a good fit. I was successful with (aspects that are similar to the job you're interviewing for), but not as strong on (parts that are different). I'm much better suited to a position like the one we're talking about today.

+ Although I did accomplish many milestones in that role, I realize I also made some mistakes. It's been a learning experience for me. What I learned was ... and I took that learning with me to my next role, where I was much more successful. For example ...

Notice how these answers begin and end with something positive, with the negative sandwiched in between. You can use this "sandwich" technique whenever you need to address something negative.

Whatever you say, it is important to say it without radiating anger, fear or shame. Work on your state of mind if you need to, perhaps with the aid of self-help books or counseling.

Don't take having been fired too seriously or personally. "Good people get fired every day," according to Tim Sackett, who runs a staffing agency. (Interesting surname, considering his occupation and the topic of his blog post!) "They get fired for making bad decisions. They get fired for pissing off the wrong person. They get fired because they didn't fit your culture. They get fired because of bad job fit." Or because of office politics.

Many of the most successful people in the world have been fired: Steve Jobs was fired from Apple, then returned years later. Oprah Winfrey, Walt Disney, Lee Iacocca, J.K. Rowling and Thomas Edison all got the boot. Look up "successful people who have been fired" online. You'll see that the list goes on and on. You're in good company.

Note: Being fired is not the same as being laid off. If your position was eliminated as part of a staff reduction, your answer is easier. You can say something like, "A business decision was made to eliminate a number of positions" – state how many, if it's a reasonably large number – "including mine." Surround this brief statement with positives as in the examples above.

"What is your greatest weakness?"

In most cases, the interviewer isn't just asking this to find out if there's a weakness that would disqualify you. They're even more interested in finding out whether you're self-aware and willing to openly discuss your shortcomings, which would indicate that you probably take feedback well. They want to hear that you are committed to continually improving your skills.

With that in mind, try talking about…

…a weakness that's closely connected to one of your greatest strengths. For example, if you're great at relationship-building and that's crucial to the job you're applying for, you might mention that you sometimes spend more time listening to a client or co-worker than you intended to. (But if it really isn't a weakness at all, it will sound evasive and insincere, so pick something else.)

…an "elephant in the room" weakness that's already very noticeable to the employer – such as having less experience than they would prefer, or a thick accent – so you have nothing to lose by bringing it up.

…a weakness you have largely overcome or that you compensate for very successfully.

No matter what weakness you bring up, keep it brief and spend more time talking about how you're overcoming it than about what a problem it is. And avoid words like "weakness" and "problem" in your answer. Use more positive words like "challenge," "growing edge" and "area where I'm growing."

Of course, don't bring up a weakness that would cause them to seriously doubt you can do the job.

Realize that certain answers – especially "I'm a perfectionist" and "I work too hard" – have been used so often they've become clichés and should be avoided, unless you can put a fresh spin on them.

"What's one area / three areas where your boss wants you to improve?"

This is similar to the question above, and can be approached similarly, but with an even more positive spin, since they're not actually asking for a negative. You can talk about things you do well but would like to do even better, or a skill that's so cutting-edge that only a really committed professional would be concerned about it. And I've heard people succeed with approaches more frank and transparent than this, as long as the issue they mention is not major and good progress is being made.

"Why is there a gap in your employment?"

Employers tend to assume that everyone wants to be employed continually. If you weren't, they may wonder what the problem was. They may imagine a serious physical or mental illness such as cancer, major depression or alcohol/ drug abuse. Or maybe that you lost your job and were unable to find a new one after many months. If other employers passed you up for a year, they may feel reluctant to take a chance on you.

First, address how the gap started. Read the tips under "Why did you leave your job?" or "Have you been fired?" above. If the situation is not likely to recur, explain why – for example, that you were caring for an ill family member who has now recovered or for whom other caregivers have been secured.

Talk about any positive activities you were engaged in, such as travel, education or volunteer work. You want to show that you're energetic and like to work, learn and grow.

If you are unemployed and haven't worked in several months, I recommend you start participating in updating your skills, doing pro bono work and/or consulting now – don't put it off! – and mention those activities in your interviews.

"Tell me about a major mistake you made."

As with the "weakness" questions, the intention here is to see whether you are open to admitting, taking responsibility for and learning from your mistakes. No one wants employees who will sweep their mistakes under the rug or blame them on others. They also want to hear that you clean up after yourself where possible, going the extra mile to make things right.

"On a software project I managed, a certain manager didn't come to the regular meetings until the final one where everyone was supposed to sign off. There, at the last minute, he objected to a great new feature the team was excited about. Later I realized how I could have countered that objection, but at the time it caught me by surprise, I didn't make a good case for it, and the feature was left off. What I learned for the future was to always make sure the key stakeholders are involved early, and that's what I've done since then. Anyway, I worked hard to ensure that the new feature would be in the next release – and it was!"

"What would you look to accomplish in the first 30/60/90 days?"

This question is typically asked of sales, managerial and executive candidates, among others. It tends to occur late in the interview process. Preparing a written plan to present is a good idea, as described in Chapter 11, "Something Extra." If other candidates don't do this and you do, you'll stand out.

Your plan should demonstrate that you have learned from your previous interviews with this company, done additional homework and understand the company and its priorities, that you will get up to speed quickly, put in extra time, respect and learn from those who have been there longer, and add value soon after hire.

"Tell me how you handled a difficult situation."

This is a behavioral interview question; it requires you to tell a story. The employer is hoping the story will show that you have skills and strengths like resourcefulness, creative problem solving ability, emotional intelligence, resilience, team leadership skills, diplomacy, staying calm and rational under pressure, and possibly technical skills as well.

Avoid using an example where you were the *cause* of the difficulty! At the same time, don't blame anybody else. Remember to be tactful; don't "talk down" your past company, boss or co-workers.

As in any story, make sure you include the successful results, which in this case might be that you prevented or at least reduced the damage that could have occurred, and that you maintained morale and good relationships. Point out how you learned from the situation and implemented measures to prevent future occurrences.

"Give me an example of a time you had to deal with an angry customer or client."

Most of us have dealt skillfully with an angry customer, or an upset co-worker, or a very anxious client.

What many of us have trouble doing is explaining *how* we did it. Often our people skills are somewhat unconscious; we may have "helped the person calm down" but we don't know how.

If you've ever had formal training in handling difficult interactions – for example, in customer service training – review that in your mind and apply the concepts and language to the incident you're remembering. This will help you describe it, as well as demonstrating that you have tools for such situations.

If you don't have such training, review the situation carefully in your memory. What did you say or do that worked? Did telling the person "Calm down" help? (Usually it doesn't.) Did listening help? (Usually it does.) What else did you say or do?

What was the outcome? Try to say more than just "He calmed down and was pleased." What did you specifically observe that tells you he was pleased? Did he stop yelling and thank you, renew his subscription, give you a "10" in a survey later, write a letter to your manager?

Show empathy for the customer in the way you tell this

story. If you don't feel any empathy for them, dig deeper – or tell a different story.

"Tell me about a time when you went above and beyond requirements."

Companies want employees and leaders who consistently go above and beyond. If you're having trouble thinking of examples, think of various projects and situations in which you excelled and showed great dedication, and ask yourself whether *everything* you did was really required.

Sometimes going above and beyond means taking the lead. One recent graduate told the story of a school project on which the work was delayed due to a conflict between team members. She took the initiative to assign each team member a role and tasks that fit their individual abilities. As a result, the project was completed on time and received an excellent grade.

"What do you know about our company?"

This is where you need to have done some research, preferably going beyond simply skimming the website. Show that you know not only the basics of the company history, leadership, products and culture, but also understand its competitive position, financial condition, challenges and opportunities, and recent news coverage.

Common related questions are "Who is our CEO?" and "Who are our competitors?"

"What are your salary expectations?"

Answering this question too specifically can lose you a lot of money, or an opportunity. Naming a figure that's too low can result in a lower offer, or even loss of the opportunity if your answer creates doubt about your value. A figure that's too high can immediately disqualify you.

This is one of the few questions where formulaic, memorized verbiage may be the best approach.

First, as soon as you apply for a job make sure you understand the range of typical salaries for the position and geographic area, because this may be one of the first questions you will be asked in a phone screen, which could happen at any time.

You can research salaries via websites like Salary, Payscale, Glassdoor, Indeed, CareerOneStop, JobSearchIntelligence, via a simple Google search, and sometimes via word of mouth. Use more than one source, since a broader range may give you more negotiating flexibility.

When the question is asked, respond with "Can you tell me what range you have budgeted for the position?"

If they tell you a range, say something like, "That seems like a reasonable ballpark. I'm sure once we agree I'm the right person for the job, we'll be able to agree on a salary that's fair."

If they won't state their range and put the question back onto you, say something like, "I've done some research and I'm seeing salaries anywhere from X to Y. I'm sure once we agree I'm the right person for the job we'll be able to agree on a salary that's fair."

"How much are/were you making at your current/ previous job?"

There are a couple of options here. You can decline to state, saying something like "I'd rather learn more about the position and how well I fit what you're looking for, before we discuss salary issues," or "It would be difficult to compare my last salary with this position for several reasons, including that I don't have enough information about your whole package. I'm sure we can agree on compensation."

If you will be changing careers or industries, you might point out that this makes your current/recent salary less relevant.

On the other hand, if your salary has been very similar to what you expect you would be offered – or if it appears you won't be considered without providing the information – it might be best to just go ahead and give them the information. If your current salary is low, include the value of any bonuses and perks in the figure you give.

"How is your search going? Have you been having other interviews?"

There are two reasons they might be asking.

On the one hand, they may be wondering whether you're about to accept another offer. A safe answer is something like, "I've been meeting with other people and discussing various opportunities, but nothing is concrete yet."

On the other hand, if you have been unemployed for more than a few months, they may wonder whether there's some reason you aren't getting hired. They may be leery of taking a chance on someone who has been passed over by many other companies.

It's usually best to avoid identifying the other companies you've interviewed with, since they see their hiring activities as confidential. Instead refer to them generically, for example as "a few Tier One tech companies" or "several small design firms."

"Tell me about a time you disagreed with your boss."

Most managers would like their staff to speak up in a constructive way when they disagree with directives. After all, they have their hands more closely on the work and may know something the boss doesn't. The best answer here would involve a congenial disagreement in which both parties had good reasons for their opinions, you communicated yours tactfully and factually, and your input led to a better solution. It would also be acceptable if the boss didn't act on your input, as long as the story shows you accepting the decision in a professional and fully engaged manner.

If the disagreement resolved in your favor, make sure you don't sound smug about it!

"What's your availability?" or "How soon could you start?"

If you're unemployed and would like to start work immediately, you can say so, but avoid sounding like you're desperate for a paycheck ASAP! If you'd prefer a later date, say something like "I'm quite available and I'd be happy to discuss a start date that works for both of us, once we agree that my abilities and the role are a good fit."

If you're currently employed, it's reasonable to state that you'll need to give at least two weeks' notice. Since the interviewer would hope for the same consideration when you leave, he will probably respect this.

If you think some negotiation may be needed on this point, keep the discussion general and don't make a commitment. The best time to negotiate is *after* they've offered you the job.

"What motivates you / gets you up in the morning / makes you excited about Mondays?"

If you can't say "excited about Mondays" with a straight face, don't use that phrase in your answer! But do show passion for the specific challenges and rewards of the work itself – solving problems (such as?), collaborating and learning from team members (say more!), achieving goals (like what?), making a difference (how?) – rather than vague generalities like "working with people" or peripheral issues like the pay or benefits.

"How do you handle conflict at work? Please give an example."

Conflict is inevitable when two or more people are working together. Employers want to know that you can resolve conflicts – whether between you and someone else, or between two others – in a constructive way.

Most examples involve talking things over with the parties involved, but many interviewees are too vague, saying "We talked it over and resolved the issue."

Say a bit more, illustrating the communication and interpersonal skills you used. What happened in that conversation? Did you try to understand the other person's point of view? What questions did you ask? How did you listen to the answers? What did you learn from the other person that helped you resolve the problem? Did you express empathy, offer ideas, or what? And as in any story, be specific about the beneficial outcomes.

Other candidates make an even worse mistake, choosing a situation they still feel emotional about and getting emotionally "hooked" into ranting on about how bad the situation was and the awful things people did or said. Choose an example that you're sure you can describe in a completely calm and even-handed manner.

"Tell me about a time you had to work with someone you didn't like, or who didn't like you."

First of all, don't reinforce an image of yourself as someone who dislikes or is disliked by others. Reframe it as a situation where it was a challenge to work effectively with this person.

This question requires you to say something negative about a co-worker, which is generally a no-no in interviews. So be tactful by not giving any information that could identify who this person is.

Take an emotionally neutral tone. Resist the urge to kvetch, even if the interviewer encourages it by offering you sympathy.

Avoid characterizing the co-worker in judgmental terms like "Nothing was ever right as far as he was concerned" or "She wasn't a team player." Instead, describe the specific behavior objectively: "He would often make negative comments about team members" or "We needed her to provide a report every Monday, but it usually wasn't done until mid-week."

Be very brief about the difficult behavior, focusing primarily on what you did to make the best of the situation and how well it turned out. Treat this as a SOAR story, emphasizing the positive results.

"What would your boss / direct reports / teammates say about you?"

Of course you want your answer to support your key selling points and other relevant skills and strengths. The trick is not just to put the desired words into these people's mouths, but actually ask yourself how they would say it. This can lead to interesting quotes or turns of phrase that show that you're authentically answering the question that has been asked.

"What are your boss's strengths and weaknesses?"

Of course, this question is not really about your boss. It's about you: what kind of relationship you tend to have with your manager; whether you're easy to manage.

Name a few of your manager's strengths — and even if they're a terrible boss, find something to wholeheartedly admire.

Good grief, do they really expect you to talk about your bosses' weaknesses? It's a test. Don't take the bait! After praising a few strengths, say "I'd rather not comment on any weaknesses." If you think highly of your boss, close by saying so.

But don't rave about how great your boss is. That's a little like telling a date how much you adored your ex!

"What's the last book you read for fun?"

Let's assume the interviewer isn't being nosy, but just wants to get to know you better as a person. Name any book you've read within the last couple of months that supports your brand – or at least presents you as an intelligent person. If you don't read books – as many people don't, these days – mention something you read online, such as a blog.

"What are your co-worker pet peeves?" or "What makes you uncomfortable in the workplace?"

Don't use the word "pet peeve" in your response, lest it sound like you cherish your annoyances. Choose something that would displease anyone, such as co-workers who don't pull their own weight. Because this is a negative, sandwich it between positives.

> *"I'm generally very focused on my own work. Of course, like anyone I don't like to see team members not pulling their own weight. As an individual contributor it isn't my place to come down on that kind of thing, but if it's affecting my work I'll generally talk it over with them and*

see if we can resolve any issues that are getting in the way. For example…"

"What question haven't I asked you, that I should have?"

A question like this is a nice opportunity. What would you like to say that hasn't been covered yet? Do you have a great story you haven't had a chance to tell? Smile and say something like "Well, I'd love to tell you about…" Or if you're stumped, say "Actually, you've been very complete! I do have some questions for you. Is it time for that?"

The questions we've looked at so far have been quite normal – you might say, vanilla. Let's get into some of the more complex flavors – maybe a bit more nutty, maybe more of a, shall we say, *rocky road.*

CHAPTER 8

Quirky Questions: Puzzling, Stressful, Off-the-Wall or Illegal

Why is a raven like a writing desk?

– The Mad Hatter, in Lewis Carroll's *Alice in Wonderland*

The questions in this chapter are – mercifully – less common than the ones we've discussed previously. But let's make sure you're prepared for whatever comes your way.

Off-the-wall

Let's start with the friendlier questions we'll encounter in this chapter, the odd inquiries like "If you could have any superpower, what power would you choose, and why?" or "What would the title of your debut album be?"

These kinds of questions are intended to give insight into your personality and values. They also test whether you react flexibly to the unexpected.

As silly as you may find these questions, answer pleasantly and try to make your answer relevant. For example, if you're interviewing for a job where managing people is key, you might say "It's important to me to understand my team – what motivates them, what they know and don't know, and what their concerns are. So mind-reading might be useful. But I think I'd rather just talk to them!"

Puzzles

Puzzle questions may sound similarly odd, like "Why are manhole covers round?" or "How many golf balls will fit into a Boeing 747?" But the difference is that these questions may actually have right answers, or at least smarter and less-smart ones.

In the early 2000s, tech companies like Microsoft and Google led a trend in using this type of question to try to assess candidates' intelligence and creative problem-solving skills. Although the approach has lost some popularity in recent years, due to doubts about whether it works, you may still be asked this type of question.

To handle puzzle questions:

+ Don't rush into answering. Start problem-solving out loud. Ask questions, if appropriate.

+ If the first answer that comes to mind seems too easy, rethink it. There may be a trick to it.

+ On the other hand, an apparently complex problem may be simpler than it appears. If it seems to involve higher math, look for an easier solution.

- If you're stuck, examine your assumptions, one by one.

- If there seems to be no one right answer, great! That gives you the opportunity to develop a uniquely creative, memorable one.

Are you wondering about the quote at the top of the chapter? How a raven is like a writing desk? Lewis Carroll answered his own question many years after Alice in Wonderland was published: "Because it can produce a few notes, though they are very flat; and it is 'nevar' put with the wrong end in front!" ("Nevar" is "raven" spelled backwards.)

Intentionally Stressful

These questions might be asked in order to see how you react to uncomfortable and unexpected situations, and whether you're able to stay cool and deal with difficult people.

The candidate is generally not told this technique will be used. So if you find yourself hearing questions like this, realize that it may be a test. First, smile and breathe. Think of it as an interesting challenge, maybe even a sort of game, to stay utterly calm and professional and give the best possible answer.

- "What do you do that drives your boss crazy?"

    (Answer that you don't do anything that drives your boss crazy, but you're always looking to improve your skills.)

+ "How would you evaluate me as an interviewer?"

(How about "Very cautiously"! Beyond that, the correct answer depends on the job you're interviewing for.)

+ "What's the worst thing you've heard about our company?"

(If something negative has appeared in the news or is well known, tactfully acknowledge what you've seen and be prepared to discuss the issue and how you feel about it.)

Illegal

In a 2015 Harris poll, one out of five employers surveyed admitted to having unknowingly asked an interview question that was illegal.

It is illegal not to hire candidates because of their race, color, sex, religion, national origin, birthplace, age, disability or marital/family status. Questions that seek to draw out information about these subjects are illegal.

In a 2016 article, Glassdoor listed the following examples:

+ How old are you?

+ When did you graduate?

+ Are you married?

+ Are you gay?

+ Do you have children (or plan on having children)?

+ Who will take care of your children while you're at work?

+ Is English your first language?

+ Are you a U.S. citizen?

+ What country are you from?

+ Where were you/your parents born?

+ What is your religion?

+ Where do you go to church?

+ What clubs or social organizations do you belong to?

+ Do you have any disabilities?

+ How is your health?

+ How tall are you? How much do you weigh?

+ Have you ever been arrested?

+ If you've been in the military, were you honorably discharged?

I'm not an attorney, and nothing in this chapter is intended as legal advice. But I do have some suggestions for handling such questions. Let's look at three options. You could:

A. **Refuse to answer,** perhaps pointing out that the question is illegal or that it's none of their business.

B. **Draw out the underlying concern,** so that you can address it without providing the information.

C. **Provide the information.**

Let's say the interviewer asks, *"Are you married?"*

Option A: "That's illegal (or personal) and I'd rather not answer it." This answer will probably make the interviewer feel criticized and embarrassed, destroying your rapport with them and making it unlikely you'll be selected for the job. If you leave out the "illegal/personal" part and simply say "I'd rather not answer that question," they may decide you're uncooperative or hiding something, so again you won't get the job.

Option B is somewhat safer. You might say, "I'd be happy to answer that, if you could first tell me…" or "May I ask what your concern is, or how that's relevant to the job?" The interviewer may respond that they're wondering whether relocation will be a problem for your spouse, in which case you can assure them there is no issue.

There is some risk in this approach, since it may jog the interviewer's memory that their question is illegal or inappropriate. However, if you have a strategic reason not to provide the information, this may be the best option.

If you already think you know why they're asking, you could just address the supposed concern: "I think you may be concerned about whether relocation will be problem. I'd like to assure you there are no issues about that."

Option C is often the best option. "Yes, I am married. If you're concerned about the relocation, I'd like you to know I've discussed it with my husband, and he's totally on board. Living in Seattle would be a great thing for both of us. Does that address your concern?"

What if they didn't ask an illegal question, but you want to bring up one of these issues – marital status, health, etc. – on your own? You have every right to provide the information if you wish. Don't go there without a good reason, because it may make interviewers anxious about the potential of a lawsuit.

Some of these items may be worth bringing up. For example, if you have a noticeable disability or health issue, you may want to proactively assure the employer that it doesn't limit your ability to do an excellent job.

In this chapter and the last, you've learned a lot about answering questions. But there's one absolutely crucial question we haven't explored yet, and it's a question that's asked toward the end of nearly every interview: *"What questions do you have for me?"*

First impressions are important, but so are endings. Failing to respond with several good questions can shoot down even a high-flying interview as quickly as you can say "No."

What are the best (and worst) questions to ask? What else do you need to know? That's our next topic.

CHAPTER 9

Asking the Right Questions (& Not the Wrong Ones!)

Judge a man by his questions rather than his answers.

– Voltaire

As you know, you need to ask questions in an interview to help you decide whether you want the job.

But it's also true that asking good questions may be necessary to *get the offer!* Why?

First, employers prefer candidates who show an interest this way. A candidate who is not inquisitive can seem not only unmotivated, but perhaps unintelligent and definitely unprepared.

The second reason is that asking questions – especially if you can do it earlier in the interview – can arm you with information that helps you market yourself. The more you know about the employer's challenges, goals and environment, the better you can target your message.

What makes a question a good one?

A good question…

> … Demonstrates communication skills, social savvy and good judgment.

> … Shows you're strongly interested in the job.

> … Demonstrates that you're thinking about how you can add value.

> … Is usually not answerable with a "yes" or "no." Open-ended questions lead to a more friendly, informative conversation.

> … Is appropriate for your industry and level. An interviewer may expect very bold questions from a corporate executive, but not from a clerical candidate.

> … Is asked in the right tone, at the right time, of the right person. Some questions require sensitive handling; for example, questions about the person who previously held the position.

> … Sounds natural, not "canned" – even if you found the question on a list like this one!

> … Shows that you've done some research on the company.

Do your homework before asking questions.

Researching the company thoroughly before the interview shows diligence and motivation. The information you gain enables you to dispense with basic questions like "How long has the company been in business?" and instead ask questions like, "I read in Forbes that this company is putting a new emphasis on X. How has that affected this department?"

Examples of facts you should know about the company:

- Basics of company history, size and structure (is it a subsidiary, or part of a family of companies?), mission, values and culture
- Products/services
- Company's market position and rank (Fortune 100/500? best/only/first of its kind?) and competitors
- Recent organizational changes, other positions currently open that may affect you (for example, your prospective manager's)
- Company's financial condition
- Trends in the industry

Where to find the information:

- The company's website, of course (and the site map may be a good place to start)
- News media and blogs

- Social media
- Online directories like Corporate Information and Hoovers
- Word of mouth
- Online discussion groups

If possible, use the company's product or service, and be prepared to talk about it. One candidate contacted the company's user support department with a minor issue to see how they handled it.

How many questions should you ask?

This depends on the position, the interviewer's preferences, how much time is available, and the structure of the interview. Three good questions at the end might be enough for some interviews; for others you might need to ask questions throughout the discussion *and* several at the end. Always prepare at least 10, in case some of your questions are answered during the interview. (It's generally appropriate to bring a written list and refer to it at the appropriate time.) Never get stuck with "Uh, no, you've answered them already."

What questions should you *not* ask?

"Ask not what the employer can do for you, but what you can do for the employer." Focus on the work and the environment in which you'll be doing it. Don't ask about salary, benefits, vacation, flextime or anything that may require negotiation – until *after* a firm offer is on the table (preferably in writing!).

It's also risky to ask the interviewer any personal questions, such as those about their family – even if family pictures are on display on the interviewer's desk. Mentioning facts you've seen in their LinkedIn profile should be okay – but be careful. Some people may feel self-conscious about the fact that you looked them up online. (I know, that's not logical – but then, *people* often aren't logical.)

And of course, don't ask questions that you could easily have researched on your own.

What counter-question should you always be prepared for?

"Why do you ask?" Always be able to explain what you're seeking by answering a certain question – or don't ask it.

What will you say after they answer your question?

Make it a conversation. Use your active listening skills and show that you "get it." Relate your own background to their answers. For example, if their answer gives you insight into the company's needs, say something about how you can help fulfill those needs.

Can you give me examples of good questions?

The following questions may be good, *depending on your situation.* Choose about 10 of them and *adapt them as necessary,* based on the circumstances and your own communication style.

Are they "safe questions"? Not necessarily! That depends on the people involved, the industry, company culture and how you ask – factors that I don't know as I write this. So use your best judgment.

About the company and the department:
(Many of these can be enhanced by referring to what you've found out through your research.)

+ What potential growth areas are people most excited about here?

+ How do you see this organization's strengths and weaknesses compared to its competitors?

+ How would you describe the company's culture? If the company was a person, what kind of person would it be?

+ How does the company reward successful performance?

+ What kind of person succeeds here?

+ Why do people come to work here instead of for your competitors? Why do they stay?

+ How does upper management view the role and importance of this department?

+ What's ahead for this company in the next five years, and how does this department fit into that?

+ What is this department's most urgent priority in the next (three or six) months?

+ What have been the department's achievements in the last couple of years?

+ What makes this department successful?

+ What is the rhythm to the work here? Is there a time of year you're pulling all-nighters, or is it consistent all year? Is it evenly spread throughout the week/month, or are there crunch days?

+ What are the greatest strengths of this company? And since no company is perfect, what could be improved upon?

About the manager (for clues about how you'll like working with him/her):

+ How did you join the company? What makes you stay?

+ What do you most enjoy about your work with this organization?

+ What keeps you awake at night?

+ What are some good ideas you've gotten from your direct reports, and how did they make a difference? (This may tell you how interested they are in such ideas, and whether they act on them.)

+ Will it be possible for me to meet my prospective co-workers during the interview process? (Present this as a way to flesh out your understanding of the company culture and the work. If the manager declines to have you meet the team, take it as a red flag.)

+ What recognition or rewards have your direct reports received in the past year?

+ What training and development have they received?

+ How do you prefer to communicate with your team? Through email, phone, dropping in, scheduled meetings?

+ What are your goals for this position/department?

+ How would you describe your management style? (This question is expected, and they will probably have a well-rehearsed answer, but it's still worth asking.)

+ What kind of person fits best with your management style? (This indirect question may elicit a more revealing answer.)

+ How will you and I work together to make me successful in this role?

About the position:

+ Who does this position report to? When would I be meeting him or her?

+ What would you consider to be the most important aspects of this job?

+ What are the most crucial skills and strengths you want to see in the person hired for this position?

+ What would a very successful (next year) look like for this company, and how does this position help achieve those goals?

+ It can be hard to get funding to hire someone these days. Why does the company see this position as crucial and worth the money?

+ How would you describe a typical week/day in this position? A typical client or customer?

+ What is the typical work week? Is overtime expected?

+ Why is this position open?

+ Is this a new position? If not, what did the previous employee move on to?

+ What types of skills do you *not* already have onboard that you're looking to bring in with the new hire?

About expectations and evaluation:

+ Thinking back to people who've been in this position previously, what differentiated the ones who were good from the ones who were really great?

+ If you were to hire me now, and a year from now give me a stellar performance review, what will I have done to earn it?

+ What are the most immediate challenges I would be facing in this position?

+ What would be the highest priority for the next six months?

+ What are the performance expectations for this position in the first year?

+ What were the major strengths of the last person who held this job, and is there anything you would like to see the new employee do differently?

+ How will my performance be reviewed, and when does that occur?

+ What are the specific criteria upon which I would be evaluated?

About advancement:

+ What are the career paths in this department?

+ What are the opportunities for training and development within this position?

+ Are lateral moves available to provide broader experience?

+ Assuming I were successful in this role, what opportunities might there be for eventual advancement?

+ How much assistance are employees given in developing their careers here?

+ Where have successful employees advanced to from this position?

About your strengths and weaknesses as a candidate:
(Ask these questions with care and with a smile, late in the interview process. They can yield very valuable information, but can also make some interviewers nervous.)

+ Now that we've talked a while, what do you see as my greatest strengths for this position?

+ On the other hand, do you have any concerns, or is there anything you see as an area for growth?

+ Is there any reason you would *not* hire me for this position?

+ If I could add/change anything about myself and my experience to make me a better fit for the position and the company, what would it be?

About a question that you're not sure how to respond to:

+ Before I answer that, may I ask you…

About the next steps:

+ What are the next steps in the process? (A *very important question.* You need to know what to expect!)
+ When should I expect to hear from you next?
+ I'd like to give you a call next week to check in and offer any additional information that might be helpful. Is there a good day for me to do that?
+ What can I do to prove to you that I'm the right person for this job?

What else?

A question is a tool. Picking the right tools for the situation is important, and so is using them well. Practice your questions as you practice other aspects of the interview. Then enjoy an interview that feels like a stimulating conversation and shows you as a sharp, motivated professional.

Up to this point, we've focused on verbal communication, but some of the most important communication takes place nonverbally: in your face, your gestures, your appearance, items you might bring to the interview, and the nervousness or confidence you exude. The next three chapters will show you how to master these aspects of interviewing. Let your actions speak as positively as your words.

SECTION III

Nailing the Nonverbals

CHAPTER 10

More than Words Can Say: Body Language, Clothes and Other Silent Messages

What you do speaks so loudly that I cannot hear what you say.

– Ralph Waldo Emerson

How do employers decide who to hire? A lot of it comes down to gut feelings, rapport, the "chemistry" you read about in Chapter 5. And those gut feelings are largely based on nonverbals like body language, listening, manners and appearance.

Much of this comes naturally, some of it you already know – like shaking hands, smiling and wearing an appropriate outfit – but I'm sure you'll find a few surprises.

Body Language

It's commonly said that most of the communication in a conversation happens nonverbally. So you'll want to get it right!

What are the biggest body language mistakes job seekers make? In a 2016 survey commissioned by CareerBuilder, U.S. hiring managers named the following mistakes (listed in order of how many managers mentioned each one):

- **Failing to make eye contact.** A full 67% of these managers reported they would be less likely to hire someone who doesn't look them in the eye. Too little eye contact can make a candidate seem insincere or insecure. Too much can feel domineering. If you make eye contact about 30-60% of the time – less when talking, more when listening – you should make a good impression.

- **Failing to smile.** Two points in the interview definitely call for a smile, to show friendliness and enthusiasm: at the beginning and the end. In between, smile when it feels natural to you, and when the interviewer smiles. (Did you know you can smile too much in an interview? A recent study by Northeastern University showed that too much smiling can give the impression you're not taking the interview seriously. In my experience, however, most people are more likely to not smile enough.)

- **Playing with something on the table.** This is distracting, drawing attention to your nervousness.

+ **Fidgeting in your seat.** This, too, draws attention to nervousness.

+ **Bad posture.** Slouching can communicate a lack of motivation, interest and respect.

+ **Crossing your arms over your chest.** This communicates defensiveness.

+ **Playing with your hair or touching your face.** If you tend to play with your long hair, tie it back. And did you know that touching the mouth or nose is sometimes associated with lying?

+ **Weak handshake.** A full, firm handshake feels welcoming and confident.

+ **Too many hand gestures.** This was mentioned by only 11% of those surveyed. Please don't take this to mean you must never talk with your hands in interviews. A good rule of thumb is to do it about as much as the interviewer does.

+ **Too-strong handshake.** Don't ignore this because it's at the bottom of the list. This writer has often felt a bit intimidated – or physically uncomfortable – with powerful handshakes. Be sensitive to the gender and size of the person you're shaking hands with!

Most of us display some of these behaviors in interviews, and we may be unaware of it. It's a very good idea to shoot a video of yourself in a mock interview and take a good look at your body language.

What about your voice?

Another reason to video yourself is to check for these common vocal mannerisms. You may have one of these issues without being aware of it.

+ **Uptalk.** A seemingly increasing number of people, especially Millennials, tend to end their sentences with an upward inflection, as if asking a question or seeking confirmation. Surveys show many people find it annoying. Practice making your sentences end on a confident, definite, downward inflection.

+ **Vocal fry.** This is the low-pitched, creaky sound that many people, especially young women, are using these days, probably as a result of emulating celebrities like Kim Kardashian, Britney Spears or the Meredith Gray character on the TV show *Gray's Anatomy*. Overuse of vocal fry can not only be annoying but damaging to the vocal cords.

+ **Extremes: speaking too softly, too loudly, too slowly or too rapidly.** If you tend toward any of these extremes, strive for moderation!

+ **Singsong or monotone.** The Free Dictionary defines singsong speech as "A tediously repetitive rising and falling inflection of the voice." Equally tedious is the monotone, in which the voice drones on without any change in pitch. If you have either of these habits, try to bring more natural variety into the inflections and rhythms of your speaking. Listen to skilled public speakers for examples.

+ **Overuse of vocal fillers such as saying "uh," "you**

know," "like," or smacking the lips at the beginning or ending of statements. Wikipedia defines "filler" as a sound or word that is spoken to signal that you're pausing to think without giving the impression that you've finished speaking. Even the best speakers use fillers *occasionally*, but a statement with multiple fillers is like clothing littered with lint or pet hair. It's unattractive and diminishes your credibility. To overcome this:

+ **Become aware of it.** You can't fix it if you don't know you're doing it. Record yourself, or do a mock interview with a friend or coach and have them point out every filler.

+ **Replace fillers with silent pauses.** The purpose of a filler is to give you a chance to think. Practice just pausing. And maybe slow down a bit.

+ **Make eye contact, or look at your notes if you're in a phone interview.** You're more likely to use a filler when staring blankly.

+ **Try aversion therapy.** You could put a rubber band around your wrist and snap it every time you use a filler. Or practice with a friend and ask them to make a loud noise or make you start over every time you use a filler.

Create rapport by mirroring body language.

Next time you're in a coffee shop, observe two friends who are enjoying a conversation. They will naturally mimic each other's body language, speech patterns and vocabulary without being conscious of it. For example, they'll both take a sip of coffee at the same moment. This unconscious mirroring is both a cause and a result of rapport, and it helps the individuals feel more connected to each other, as if they're "on the same wavelength."

Although mirroring is usually unconscious, you can help it along intentionally. Don't be too obvious or exact about it, especially if the interviewer's gesture is not one that you as a candidate should imitate. For example, if the interviewer leans way back in his chair, you might just lean back the slightest bit – the effect is just as good.

Practice mirroring with friends first. Don't try it in interviews until you know you can make it look natural.

Listening

If you want to sound smart, listen. The more you understand the employer's interests and concerns, the better you can address them.

If you want the interviewer to like and trust you, listen to her. We all crave being listened to. And managers want employees who listen well. Listen actively. Look like you're listening. Say something occasionally that shows you've understood.

We've all heard and read so much about listening, yet we don't do it very well. Why not? Stephen Covey put it well: "Most people don't listen with the intent to understand. They listen with the intent to reply." If we're busy thinking about what we're going to say next, we aren't giving the interviewer our full attention.

By the time you read this chapter, you've probably

spent many hours preparing what you're going to say in your interviews. So when the interviewer is talking, *trust your preparation*. Let go of thinking about what you'll say. Give your undivided attention to the interviewer so that the relationship, and the dialogue, can fully develop in the moment.

Note-taking

Just like any other nonverbal behavior, taking notes sends a message about you. Asking politely if you may take notes, then quickly jotting down the occasional fact or detail, sends the message that you're well organized and make a point of keeping track of information given to you.

On the other hand, *continually* taking notes may raise questions: whether you're really listening, whether you have a problem with memory, whether you're able to think on your feet.

Laboring to take notes in full sentences, word for word, looks inefficient. Learn how to take fast, abbreviated notes. It's a skill that will serve you for the rest of your life.

Manners

An interview is more formal than most day-to-day situations, so watch your manners from the moment you're within eyeshot of the building until you've left the area afterwards.

Here are some fine points you may not have thought of:

- Arriving more than 15 minutes early is awkward for everyone involved. It's great to get to the area far in advance to be sure you won't be late, but wait in a coffee shop or in your car until the last few minutes. Use the extra time to review your notes, do relaxation exercises or visualize a successful interview.

- Wait to be offered a seat before sitting down, or at least until others have taken their seats.

- Don't place personal items on the interview table, other than a notepad and pen. Place your briefcase or purse on the seat next to you, or on the floor under your chair.

- As of 2017, taking notes on an electronic device at an interview is generally frowned upon. Cell phones are taboo, and note-taking on a laptop is too obtrusive, too audible, and creates a feeling of a barrier between you and the interviewer. "The jury is still out" regarding use of other devices such as tablets.

- About cell phones: It's not enough to turn the phone off. It must be *out of sight* to eliminate even the *appearance* that you might take a call during the interview.

- When leaving the interview, if possible stop in the outer office and thank the person who greeted you when you arrived.

And a word about names: Most people like to hear their own name, so use it when shaking hands at the beginning and end of the interview, and maybe once or twice in between. So, will it be "John" or "Mr. Jones"?

The etiquette on this is changing, and not everyone agrees on it. In the *Harvard Business Review* in 2011, communication and leadership consultant Jodi Glickman wrote, "Addressing people by their first name is now the norm in corporate America," but later in the same article she wrote, " It may be counterintuitive to look a powerful CEO in the face for the first time and call them boldly by their first name. And it may be hard as that CEO to swallow it."

One common view is that it's best to follow the interviewer's cues: if they call you by your first name, reply in the same way. Others say it's better to address the interviewer as Mr. or Ms. (or another title they prefer, if you have any way of knowing that) until they specifically invite you to use their first name.

Since there is no one definitive answer, we each have to use our own best judgment.

Appearance

Before you ever answer "Tell me about yourself," you have already told the interviewer how you feel about yourself and the opportunity. You've told them how much respect you have, or don't have, for them and their company. You've told them whether you understand their world – whether you "get it."

All of that is instantly communicated by your outfit and grooming.

Over thousands of years of evolution, human beings have evolved to make snap judgments. Our hunter-gatherer ancestors faced life-and-death struggles routinely, whether from huge animals or other people. Those who could quickly size up an adversary with reasonable accuracy, survived and reproduced.

We still make those instant judgments, based on body language and appearance. It may not be very enlightened, but it's how we are.

If that doesn't seem fair, or if you dislike business clothes and prefer to do the bare minimum to play the game, believe me, I sympathize. Personally, I look and feel better in jeans than in a suit. Nevertheless, *those who play the game well, win.* Besides, knowing you're perfectly attired can be a huge boost to your confidence.

So here are the recommended moves in this appearance game.

Interview attire in the vast majority of workplaces is conservative. The advice below is geared towards that majority, but realize that the rules are different according to the job, industry and region. If you're interviewing for a job in a "creative" field such as advertising or fashion, for example, you'll want to look more creatively stylish than if you're interviewing at a financial firm.

As a general rule, interview attire should be a step up from the way you would dress on the job.

+ **If the workplace is casual (let's say, the jeans and T-shirts of Silicon Valley software engineers):** For the interview, dress in "business casual." This is a deceptive term, because business casual is *not* what most of us would call casual. For men, business casual means slacks with a crease, an open collared shirt (no tie) and maybe a blazer. For women, it's similar except you have the option of replacing the slacks with a knee-length skirt, and the shirt with a blouse. Both men and women should wear closed-toe business shoes.

+ **If business casual is the standard daily attire (as in many offices today):** Wear a suit to the interview – preferably blue or gray, with closed toe dress shoes, and if you're a man put on a tie.

+ **If you'll be wearing a suit on the job every day:** Clearly that's what you'll be wearing to the interview!

When in doubt, ask the recruiter who scheduled the interview for their advice about what to wear.

It's best to carry only one item: a briefcase or portfolio to hold your resumes, notepad and so on. For a woman to carry both a briefcase and a purse may give a disorganized impression; better to use a smaller purse that will fit inside your briefcase.

What about self-expression? It's great to be real and interesting and let people know who you are. To express your personality while still radiating impeccable professionalism can be a challenge, but if you can pull it off, all the better! But do avoid loud colors or anything startling, eccentric, sexy or otherwise distracting. Keep the focus on your professional self.

Groom for success. For hair, neat and tidy is essential. If your hair is long, pulling it back or up may be the best way to ensure it looks businesslike. For women, light makeup is best and looks more professional than going without. For men, a clean-shaven look is best, despite the current popularity of "designer stubble" and beards.

Both sexes should avoid using any scented personal care products, especially perfumes and colognes, since many people have unpleasant physical reactions to these.

Hygiene must be flawless, of course. Avoid strong-smelling foods, coffee and alcohol, which can leave unwelcome smells. If you smoke, do everything you can to prevent tobacco smell on your clothes, hair, hands or breath.

As of this writing in 2017, tattoos and piercings (other than women's pierced ears) are still considered beyond the pale for most interviews. If you can't cover all your tats with clothing, there are makeup products such as DermaBlend designed to hide them.

Look right, sound right and nail all your nonverbals so you're sending a consistent message in every medium: *that you're the best person for the job.*

Appropriate clothes and nonverbals are a must – but often it's what's *not* required that really makes you stand out. What can you bring to the interview to *not just tell, but show* your value to the employer?

CHAPTER 11

Something Extra: Portfolios, Presentations and Plans

Tell me and I forget, show me and I may remember, involve me and I learn.

– paraphrase of ancient Chinese proverb

Prove it.

– anonymous (Who hasn't said this?)

There are no traffic jams along the extra mile.

– Zig Ziglar

You're at the interview to **educate** – to memorably teach the employer about your value. And it's well known that people remember information better when it includes visuals.

You're also there to **persuade**. Don't just *claim* you have certain skills and qualities. Look for ways to offer *evidence*.

And you're there to **stand out.** So look for opportunities to offer something *extra* that the other candidates might not.

Used correctly, "extras" such as portfolios, presentations and 30/60/90-day plans can help you educate, persuade and stand out in the interviewer's mind.

Portfolios aren't just for artists.

Portfolios – whether online or physical – aren't just for "creative" professionals like graphic designers and copywriters. If the quality of your work can be demonstrated by several of the following items, consider assembling them into a binder or computerized presentation.

You might include:

+ Samples of work or summaries of projects (but note the warning below)
+ Writing samples
+ Kudos
+ Awards
+ Letters of recommendation (or better yet, printouts of LinkedIn recommendations)
+ Positive performance reviews
+ Graphs, charts or other infographics
+ Certificates, licenses or transcripts
+ Resume, cover letter and references

* And what else? Use your imagination and good judgment.

Be *very careful* not to violate your past employers' confidentiality – nor even to *appear* to do so. Work samples, writing samples and performance reviews can contain highly sensitive or proprietary information.

If you provide recommendations from others, be aware that the employer may reach out to them for a reference. See Chapter 14 for suggestions on preparing your contacts for such calls.

Use an attractive binder – don't skimp! – and place each item in a page protector, perhaps with copies to share behind each original. Better yet, design the portfolio as a copy to be given to the interviewer. Do not impose on them to return it to you afterwards.

If you have only one item or two extra items to show, for example a letter of recommendation and a list of references, you can simply provide these to the interviewer along with your resume.

Consider giving a mini-presentation with your tablet or laptop.

Some interviews require that you give a presentation – but if it's not required, why not be the only candidate who prepared one anyway?

This can be especially effective if presentation skills are relevant to the job, or if some of your skills – for example, web design – lend themselves well to an online presentation.

Do not ask to use the employer's presentation equipment. Keep your use of technology simple and seamless. A tablet computer may be the best choice, because it's easy to hand back and forth. And make sure your battery is fully charged; don't search around for an outlet to plug into.

Any unasked-for presentation should be very brief. It could be anywhere from a quick reference to one particularly telling infographic, or a multi-slide presentation the length of a typical interview answer (which you may recall, I suggest limiting to a minute or two).

Introduce the presentation as a way of answering a question that has been asked. "To answer that question, I'd like to show you a one-minute presentation I've prepared on my tablet. All right?"

Remember that applications like PowerPoint, Keynote, Prezi or Google Slides are only as effective as your use of them. Spend at least a few minutes reading up on smart presentation design in terms of font sizes, balance of text versus images, color and so on.

A 30/60/90-day plan is appropriate for certain occupations.

This tool is typically used by executives, managers and sales or marketing professionals, but it could be effective for others as well. The plan shows what you would accomplish in your first three months on the job, and the purpose is to demonstrate that you fully understand the role, have good ideas about how to perform it and are driven to excel in it.

Craft and present this toward the end of the interview process, after completing at least an interview or two, when you've gained detailed knowledge of the challenges, resources and expectations involved in the position.

Expect to spend a number of hours researching the company and its environment, writing the plan and developing a polished document or electronic presentation.

Since you're not yet on the job, the plan will probably be tentative, and may include mention of additional information you would seek or alternative courses of action to be considered. At the interview, engage the interviewer in discussion about your plan and invite feedback.

Be deferential in introducing extras into the interview.

Remember that the employer is in charge of the agenda for the interview and respect that. You want to bring your portfolio, presentation or plan into the meeting only with their permission, at the right moment and without disrupting the smooth flow of the meeting.

Physical portfolio, plan or other document: If the interview is taking place at a conference table, you might say something like, "May I set this here?", making it natural for the interviewer to ask you about it when they're ready. Otherwise, wait until a topic arises that corresponds to what you've brought and ask, "May I show you something that relates to this?"

Electronic presentation: It may be distracting or seem inappropriate to have your device in plain sight before you've had a chance to explain its presence. It may be best to keep it in your briefcase until the right moment has arisen and the interviewer has agreed to view your presentation.

Be prepared for the possibility that the interviewer may not want to look at what you've prepared, either due to time constraints or a desire to be "fair" by following the same format with each applicant. In that case, you might offer a hard copy or attach it with your follow-up correspondence afterwards. Your effort was not wasted – you've still demonstrated your exceptional motivation, creativity and work ethic.

It's not just what you *say* that counts in the interview – nor even how you look and what you bring – but also *how you are*: nervous and stiff, or calm and confident. The next chapter is so important we could very well have opened the book with it.

CHAPTER 12

Calm and Confident – Here's How

Whether you think you can or you think you can't,
you're right.

– Henry Ford

It's perfectly normal to be nervous about job interviews. But if you get so anxious that your voice shakes, you can't stop fidgeting or you find it hard to think clearly, that's a problem. Fortunately, there's a lot you can do about it.

Too often we feel like we have no control over our anxieties, no way to consciously cultivate confidence. Abundant research shows this is just not true. In this chapter you'll learn several ways to calm your nerves and feel confident.

Psychoanalyst Anna Freud wrote, "I was always looking outside myself for strength and confidence, but it comes from within. It is there all the time." The following practical tips and techniques can help you find that inner confidence. Experiment – find out which of these tools work best for you, and then use them!

Breathing and Other Relaxation Techniques

Psychologist Fritz Perls once said, "Fear is excitement without the breath." This may be an oversimplification, but some of your nervousness may actually be excitement about the opportunity. Your excitement is an asset, since it shows you're passionate about the job.

So appreciate your excitement, and then breathe to release the anxiety. Easier said than done?

Here are a couple of quick, easy breathing exercises from a Harvard Medical School blog. Try them right now.

Breathing with a peaceful phrase:
1. While sitting comfortably, take a slow deep breath, quietly saying to yourself "I am" as you breathe in and "at peace" as you breathe out.

2. Repeat slowly two or three times.

3. Feel your entire body let go into the support of your chair.

Abdominal breathing:
1. Place your hand just beneath your navel so you can feel the gentle rise and fall of your belly as you breathe.

2. Breathe in. Pause for a count of three.

3. Breathe out. Pause for a count of three.

4. Continue like this for one minute.

Notice how you feel before and after doing these exercises.

You can also use your imagination to help you relax. Try these techniques and see which one works best for you.

Color visualization:

1. Think of a color that you find relaxing.

2. As you breathe slowly and deeply, imagine that you're breathing that color into various areas of your body. Feel the color bringing relaxation wherever it goes.

Rubber bands visualization:

1. Focus on a tense area such as your neck or shoulders, and imagine that the area is made of taut rubber bands stretched in between pegs.

2. Now imagine the pegs are released and the rubber bands go limp. Feel the relief.

Whatever technique you prefer, practice it often and enjoy it. Make it part of your everyday life so it comes naturally to you when you need it – like in the waiting area right before an interview.

Growing Your Confidence

If you're like most people, your level of confidence changes fluidly from day to day, and even from minute to minute. The good new is this: if it's so fluid, that means it's *changeable* and you can change it intentionally.

Here are several ways to feel more confident in your job search:

Act the way you want to feel. As you practice for interviews, and in the interview itself, do and say everything as if you were confident. You'll begin to actually feel that way. Use confident language: "I'm confident" or "I'm convinced" rather than "I think" or "I feel." Avoid saying you "tried to" do this or that. As Yoda said in *The Empire Strikes Back*, "Do not try. Do. Or do not. There is no try."

Use power poses. Here's a great example of how "acting the way you want to feel" works. Research done at Harvard University has shown that adopting a confident pose for only two minutes alters a person's hormone balance, making them feel more confident. Try the "Wonder Woman" or "Superman" pose – stand up straight with your legs apart and your hands on your hips for two minutes. You might combine this with a breathing exercise such as those above and get multiple benefits at one time.

Yoga and martial arts include many poses that radiate confidence and strength, while encouraging deep breathing and improving posture. Many people have experienced increased confidence as a result of these practices.

Exercise. Countless job seekers have found that an exercise habit boosts confidence. Regular exercise brings energy, well-being, a sense of accomplishment and a feeling of control over one's body and mind, not to mention a healthier appearance. If your work ethic says "I don't have time," think of it as an investment in your career success.

Don't believe everything you think. Cognitive behavioral therapy (CBT) is a very successful approach to feeling better by changing your thoughts. If you're feeling bad about yourself it's probably because of something you're thinking. Practice disputing those thoughts and replacing them with realistically positive ones. For example, when you catch yourself thinking "I'm no good at interviewing," replace that thought with "I'm improving my interview skills and I will get an offer."

Trying to *block out* negative thoughts doesn't usually work. Instead, just compassionately *notice* them and then *replace* them. This work takes patience – doing it once isn't enough – but every little bit helps.

Use Mental Imagery. It is well known that top performers in the arts, athletics and other fields use mental imagery, also known as creative visualization, to build their skills and set up the mental conditions for success. The idea is to experience, in your imagination, the way you want to feel, think, speak and act during your next interview. On some level, your brain stores this experience as *learning,* almost as if you had participated in a real, highly successful interview. Naturally, this prepares you for a confident and effective performance in the real world. This isn't magic; it's supported by scientific research. (You can look up "motor imagery" on Wikipedia.)

First relax, using any relaxation technique that works for you. Then, vividly imagine going through a very successful interview, feeling confident from start to finish. If you start to feel tense or worried, use your technique again to bring back calm and confidence before you continue. Be sure to give your "mental movie" a happy ending!

Do this for a few minutes every day. If you find it hard to concentrate on your imagery, work with a coach or therapist who has skills in guided visualization. Ask them to make you a recording you can listen to again and again. (This is part of the service I offer to my coaching clients, and it can be done remotely.)

Start a kudos file. Gather up or write down any praise you've received about your work, whether it was as casual as a comment or as formal as a performance review or LinkedIn recommendation. (If you don't have LinkedIn recommendations, ask several people to give you one!) Look through these things when you need a boost.

If you haven't kept any of the compliments or recognition you've received in the past, make a point of doing so from now on.

If your past experience was in environments where little praise or recognition is given, I empathize with you! Many managers and companies fail to see the importance of recognizing good work. Visualize your current job search landing you in a more supportive situation!

Last but certainly not least, confidence comes from *being prepared*. Really practice what you learn from the various chapters of this book. Get thoroughly ready. If you've been "winging it" until now, you may be quite surprised at the difference this makes.

Confidence is contagious! Let your confidence in yourself convince the interviewer.

Part of being prepared is knowing what to expect. Interview formats vary widely, from a recorded video session to the "firing line" pressures of a formal panel interview, and each comes with its own challenges. You may love surprises on your birthday, but probably not in interviewing! The next chapter will help you adapt confidently to different types of interviews.

SECTION IV

Know What to Expect

CHAPTER 13

Twelve Types of Interviews

*Expect the unexpected, and whenever possible
be the unexpected.*

– Lynda Barry

The classic one-on-one, in-person meeting is only one of the many forms an interview can take. You may encounter a range of formats, from recorded interviews to meal interviews and more. Each type of interview has its own challenges and opportunities. This chapter will help you understand how to succeed with all of them.

How do you know the format of your upcoming interview? Usually, the human resources person who schedules the interview will tell you if it's not just a traditional one-on-one. If it's not clear, ask. For example, if they tell you you'll be meeting with five people at once, ask "So it's a panel interview?" (And ask for each person's name and role, too.)

Phone Screening

A screening can be a lot like a "pop quiz," occurring when you least expect it. Don't be caught off guard. As soon as you've sent a resume, get ready.

First of all, make sure you have a clear, professional voicemail greeting that includes your name. Don't make a recruiter wonder whether their confidential message will be heard by the right person.

When you hear that voice saying "I'm calling about the opening at X Company," you don't want to be struggling to remember "Which job was that? What did I tell them about myself?" Make sure the following information is instantly available near the phone, or in your purse or briefcase.

+ Job announcements you've applied to recently

+ Resumes and cover letters

+ Your REV Intro outline, unless you have it memorized

+ Appointment calendar, if you don't use your cell phone for this

+ Notepad and pen

The recruiter may be anxious to "talk for a few minutes right now" even though it's not a good time for you. If there are several good candidates available, asking to reschedule may put you at a disadvantage. But if it's really a bad time, it may be better to say "Can we talk a bit later, maybe in 15 minutes?" – rather than interview badly because you just woke up or are about to go into another important meeting.

Along with general questions like "Tell me about yourself" and "Why are you interested in this job?", you may be asked about your current/past salary or your salary expectations. See Chapters 3 and 7 for help with these questions.

One advantage of a phone interview is that you can refer to notes if you need to, such as your REV Intro outline or SOAR stories list. Spread the notes out in front of you so you don't need to handle them, to avoid rustling noises.

You might think body language is unimportant in a phone interview, but actually the interviewer can hear whether you're smiling. To help you remember to smile, draw a smiley face on your notes. And sit up straight or stand up, which makes your voice sound more energetic.

One on One, Face to Face

This is the classic interview format. Typically longer than a phone screening, an in-person interview may be a half hour, an hour or even longer (which is usually a good sign).

You can learn a lot from physically being there in the office. Look around and pay attention for clues about the company culture and what it's like working there. Be friendly, but not too chatty, with the receptionist and whoever else you encounter.

Panel Interview

Panel interviews are also sometimes known as committee or departmental interviews. They are often very firmly structured as to the questions asked, order of the questions, and even the seating arrangements.

These interviews can feel very artificial and "stiff." But look at it this way: the interviewers probably don't enjoy it either. Let that thought give you a feeling of empathy toward them! Be gracious, put them at ease, and you may end up making yourself feel more relaxed as well.

Address all of the interviewers as you answer each question, not just the person who asked. Strive for a friendly rapport with everyone, including the least friendly person, and especially the decision maker.

Write down the name and role of each person present. (Do this in advance if possible.) Arrange the names on your notepad in the same way that the people are arranged in the room – Brenda on the left, Carlo on the right, etc. Ask for business cards so you'll have contact information to follow up with everyone individually.

Group Interview

The term "group interview" can mean different things, but what we'll focus on here is a process where multiple candidates interact together in a round-table discussion or small-group exercise.

This format allows interviewers to observe interpersonal skills such as teamwork, leadership, and helping to facilitate the stated goals of the exercise.

It's a balancing act: demonstrate your skills without taking over; collaborate with people who may also be your competitors – as you might do on the job, if you were competing with teammates for a promotion while still working together for a common goal.

Sometimes "group interview" simply means meeting

with more than one person at a time, for example the hiring manager plus a few team members. As in a panel interview, use eye contact to include everyone in your answers, and of course give extra attention to the person who may become your boss.

Behavioral Interview

A behavioral interview, also known as a performance-based interview, is one where most of the questions will start with language like "Tell me about a time when…" and require you to tell a specific story from your work experience.

The theory is that a person's behavior in the past is the best predictor of how they will perform if hired. So, as emphasized in Chapter 2 and throughout this book, it's important to develop a written list of success stories.

You won't necessarily be told "This will be a behavioral interview," since performance-based interviewing is used, at least to some extent, in most interviews.

Sequential or All-day Interview

Multiple interview rounds are increasingly common. When they're crammed into one day it can be overwhelming.

Keeping your energy up is one of the challenges here. If you're among those of us who don't function well without frequent fuel, ask when there will be breaks in the interviewing and bring food. If time permits, a quick walk around the block may help refresh you between meetings.

Varying the stories you tell is important. Interviewers may compare notes later, and you don't want them to discover you told the exact same stories every time, as if that's all you have to say.

Don't let all the interviews blur together in your mind. If possible, take a few notes between meetings: questions that were asked, stories you told, what you learned about each interviewer. This will help you write smart, personalized thank-you notes later.

Meal Interview

It may not be called an interview, but a meal with your prospective boss and/or teammates can have a strong effect on your candidacy, so prepare as you would for an interview. In addition, if you know the name of the restaurant in advance, look up the menu online and plan your order beforehand.

Eat very little so that you're free to talk. Avoid alcoholic beverages, even if the boss is drinking. Keep your phone switched off and out of sight. Be nice to your server.

Meal interviews tend to include more small talk than most. One good conversation strategy is to ask the others how they came to join the company and what they enjoy most about their work there. But follow the lead of the boss: if he sticks to business, do likewise.

And of course, be on your best behavior as to conversational topics and table manners — even if others break the rules.

Video Interview

Most employers use video interviewing at times, but many people find it a bit unnatural and uncomfortable. If you can help make the experience feel more engaging and enjoyable for yourself and others, you will certainly stand out.

Video interviews may be either two-way or asynchronous. In a two-way call, you're communicating in real time, perhaps via Skype, Google Hangouts or GoToMeeting. In an asynchronous interview you'll record your responses for company employees to view later.

To ensure you'll use the technology smoothly and without stress, try it out ahead of time. If you have technical difficulties during the interview, notify the interviewer immediately.

How you look is very important, and lighting is the key. Check yourself through your computer's Photo Booth or Crazy Cam application, or through a camera or even in a mirror. Look into the camera often to create the effect of eye contact.

Case Interview

Case interviews are used in filling roles that require problem solving and analytical skills, especially management consulting and positions that require an MBA.

In a case interview, you would be presented with a problem scenario similar to those you would encounter on the job and asked to develop a solution. Candidates often spend many hours and days preparing for case interviews. Entire books have been devoted to advice on answering them effectively, and there are many sample cases and good how-to resources online.

Many of these resources are on the websites of consulting firms like Accenture and McKinsey and Company. Here are a few tips from these sites:

+ Practice many cases ahead of time, especially with others, and get feedback on how you're doing.

+ Understand that the interviewer doesn't expect to hear a perfect solution; in many cases it would take a whole team to do that.

+ Listen carefully. Interviewers may give you tips and clues.

+ Don't jump into answering right away. Take a minute to think about the case, ask questions and plan your answer.

+ Show your thought processes. Use a whiteboard if one is available. The interviewer is interested in how you approach, structure and communicate your answer.

Stress Interview

In the "Common Questions" chapter I listed several "stress questions" that are intended to test interviewees ability to perform effectively under uncomfortable circumstances or with difficult people. In addition to questions like "How would you rate me as an interviewer?", the interview may be designed to be stressful in other ways as well.

Stress tactics may include asking you the same question repeatedly, as if your answer was inadequate or they don't believe you. They may sigh, frown continually, avoid eye contact, interrupt or act as if they're not listening. They may act hostile or rushed.

It may be hard to tell whether the interviewer always acts this way – a serious concern if they will be your manager – or whether it's just an interview technique. One tip-off is if the interviewer's manner suddenly changes at the end, becoming more friendly.

The key to success in this type of interview is to stay calm and respond with impeccable professionalism. Don't take the behavior personally. View the situation as an interesting challenge. Remember to smile – it may actually make you feel better as well as demonstrate your unflappability.

If the stress tactics are extreme, you may want to ask in a pleasant tone whether you are being tested for your ability to handle stress, and whether that indicates that the position is typically very stressful.

If the interviewer's behavior makes you uncertain whether you want the job, set that thought aside and think about it after you leave. If you make a hasty negative decision during the interview you may regret it later when you weigh the factors more calmly.

Job Fair

Standing at a company's booth, you chat with a company representative for maybe five minutes, hand them your resume and the encounter ends. Unbeknownst to you, after you leave they write a note on the resume that determines whether you will be contacted for a phone screening or a more formal interview.

Was this five-minute conversation an interview? You bet it was!

Here's what you need to do to succeed in these mini-interviews:

+ Dress as you would for any interview.

+ Be knowledgeable about the company and any suitable open positions listed on their website.

+ Show enthusiasm and passion.

+ Don't give the impression their company is just one random stop, or that you're applying everywhere. If you're applying at other booths nearby, don't be obvious about it. It looks better to approach a booth from elsewhere in the fair, as if you've gone out of your way.

Testing and Projects

As hiring processes become increasingly rigorous, testing at interviews has become more common and diverse, including written tests of basic skills such as writing or math, job skills, personality, management style and so on. Testing of skills in using Microsoft Word, Excel or workplace equipment are common. You may be asked to work your way through an in-box or prepare and deliver a presentation. Find out as much as possible about any tests that will be required. Study, and take practice tests online, even for personality tests.

If required to take a drug test, be aware that false positive results can occur if you have recently taken certain medicines, such as ibuprofen, cold and allergy remedies, diet pills or sleeping aids, or eaten foods containing poppy seeds or hemp.

Work projects may include assignments of actual work typical of the job, such as redesigning a website, writing or reviewing software code, or planning a social media campaign. You may be asked to do the work on the spot or at home.

Job seekers are sometimes suspicious of take-home projects and other lengthy assignments, and not necessarily without cause. While in most cases the assignments are honestly intended only to test the applicant's skills, some employers have gone on to profit from applicants' ideas or work. How can you protect yourself from such practices? There is no simple answer.

When asked to complete a very time-consuming project, consider how seriously the company is interested in you and how much you want the job. Research their reputation. Ask for an estimate of the time required or how much detail is expected; in some cases a fully useable product may not be required. In some cases job seekers have brought along a simple mutual nondisclosure agreement (NDA). If the employer refuses to sign, that may be a red flag.

Knowing what to expect will help you to shine in any interview format and avoid stressful surprises. The next chapter will help you avoid unpleasant surprises in another area: references. Who might the employer talk to, what will they say – and what can you do about it?

CHAPTER 14

Five Dangerous Myths about References

Unless a reviewer has the courage to give you unqualified praise, I say ignore the bastard.

– John Steinbeck

If only the management of references was as simple as the breezy quotation at the top of this page.

At some point in the interview process you'll be asked for a list of people who can provide a reference, and toward the end of the process the employer will probably check these references – and they might not stop there.

The common fallacies discussed below can derail your progress toward the offer you've worked so hard to capture. Ignore them at your peril!

Myth #1:

Employers will only contact people from the list you provide.

Many employers will contact other people as well. It's neither illegal nor particularly difficult for them to do so. They can find your past managers and co-workers via social media, websites, online directories and word of mouth. They may even find people at companies you haven't listed on your resume or application.

Myth #2:

Past employers can legally only give out your title, dates of employment and most recent salary.

Many companies do have company policies forbidding employees from giving out additional information, but that doesn't mean it's against the law. And does everybody follow company policy anyway? Don't count on it.

Myth #3:

There's nothing you can do about bad references.

First, you need to know whether bad references are occurring. If you're not sure, hire a reference checking firm like Allison & Taylor to do a reference check for you. It's not expensive.

If you suspect that a certain individual may be giving you a negative reference, pluck up your nerve and reach out to him to talk it over, preferably in person. The purpose here is to listen to his point of view, acknowledge that there may have been difficulties in the past, and explain how you've learned and grown since then. Appeal to his sympathy and point out that you need a chance to get a new start. Ask whether he would be willing to emphasize the positive aspects of your past work, or at least to avoid commenting.

If talking to him doesn't work, consider sending a firm "cease and desist" letter to someone higher up in the company. Name the person giving the negative references and ask that the reference be limited to the job title and dates of employment. Usually this will solve the problem. For more clout, it may be helpful to have the letter come from an attorney.

Myth #4:

Once someone has agreed to give you a reference, all you need to do is put them on the list and give it to the employer.

Actually, there are many ways that could go wrong. Help ensure successful outcomes by working with your reference people as follows:

1. **Ask each person if they're willing to provide a reference before you give out their name.** Ask them what they would say. If they seem uncomfortable, or if you have any sense that they would give faint praise, thank them politely anyway. But don't put them on your list.

2. **Inform them each time you give out their name.** Let them know who they will be hearing from and the nature of the job. It's no good having them rave about your management skills if you're interviewing for an individual contributor role.

3. **Help them target their comments.** Suggest specific skills, projects or accomplishments to mention. Send this information in an email so they can easily refer to it when needed. Don't expect them to keep your job search at top of mind.

4. **Make sure they'll be available – and not on vacation, for example.** If an employer leaves a message and fails to hear back, they may assume the worst: that the person is uncomfortable talking about you.

5. **Ask them to respond as quickly as possible.** Employers may take the speed of the response as an indication of how eager the person is (or isn't) to sing your praises.

6. **Check in later to verify that the conversation happened and how it went.** You may learn something important about the employer, what they're looking for and what impresses or concerns them about you.

Myth #5:

It's fine to present your references before you are asked for them.

Don't wear out a good reference on employers who are not seriously interested in hiring you. As a courtesy to your reference providers, offer their names and contact information only when required.

If you want to have contacts vouching for you earlier in the process – which is often extremely helpful – ask instead for a letter of recommendation, a LinkedIn recommendation, or, if your contact has a relationship with the employer, a phone call to put in a good word.

We're now in the last laps of the interview process, and it's a crucial time. Last impressions can be almost as important as first ones. How will you conclude your interview in a way that leaves a highly persuasive image of you in the interviewer's mind?

SECTION V

Happy Endings – and Great Beginnings

CHAPTER 15

Ending on the Right Note

Finally, in conclusion, let me say just this.

– Peter Sellers

Too often, interviewees end an interview by saying what Peter Sellers did in the quote above: basically nothing! Well, okay, nearly everybody remembers to say "Thank you." That's a good start. But why waste one of the key moments of interview "air time"?

Why is it key? Because people tend to remember what came first, and what came last. So rise above the mumble-and-stumble exits of your competitors by preparing a closing statement that reinforces your positive image, your brand and your key selling points.

Here's what you want to accomplish:

1. Convey appreciation for the interview.
2. Leave your REV points clearly fixed in the interviewer's mind.

3. Express enthusiastic interest in the job.

Once the interviewer has finished with his questions and answered yours, it's time. Before you get up to leave, make a brief closing statement that nails these three objectives.

Appreciation

Obviously, it's only polite to thank the interviewers for taking the time to meet with you. Show special appreciation for anything extra the interviewer has done, such as coming in early or staying late for the interview, taking you to lunch or giving you a tour of the office.

> *"Michael, thank you so much for meeting with me today. I've really enjoyed talking with you. And thanks for taking the time to show me around. I'm very glad I was able to meet Raj and Irene. I've gotten a great impression of the whole team."*

REV Points Revisited

At the beginning of the interview you answered the "Tell me about yourself" inquiry with an introduction that emphasized your REV (Relevant, Exceptional and Verifiable) selling points, the top factors you thought would make you stand out to the interviewer as the right person to hire. At that time, you didn't know for sure what the interviewer would consider most crucial. To some extent, it was guesswork.

By the end of the interview you may know better.

Maybe the interviewer's eyes lit up about some of your REV Points more than others. Maybe the job matches your skills in a way you hadn't realized before. So update your key selling points into a very brief statement of the great fit between you and this job.

Here's an example based on Denise, the sales manager mentioned early in the book:

> *"From what you've described about your plans, my ability to capitalize on change and deliver results quickly fits really well with your goal of expanding into your new global markets. And I was excited to discover today that you need the new hire to build a larger team, because as I've said, I did hire and lead a very successful new team at Top Tier, and I'm sure I can drive equally strong results for you here."*

Expressing Interest / Asking for the Job

One of the pet peeves of interviewers is when the applicant leaves the interview without expressing a strong interest in the job. Don't make the mistake of thinking they'll *assume* you're interested. For all they know, you may have changed your mind based on something you heard during the meeting.

If there will be an additional round of interviews, make it clear you're excited about meeting again.

If this is the last interview, say you want the job, even if you're not sure you do. You can always decline later, but don't shut the door prematurely by seeming unenthusiastic.

Asking for the job might sound like this:

"I know I can deliver what you're looking for, and the role is ideal for me. I'd really like to work with you and your team."

Depending on what has been said about the next steps, you may want to follow that with one of these questions:

"What's the next step?"

"I'm looking forward to hearing from you."

"Have I given you all the information you need to offer me the job?"

"Is there anything else I can do to make you completely confident that I'm the right candidate?"

"On a scale of one to ten, how do you think I'd do in this job? ... Is there anything I could do to make that a ten?"

Notice that those last two questions invite the interviewer to give you an evaluation of your suitability for the job (but not your interviewing skills – don't expect them to play career coach!). If you receive a candid response, the feedback may create an opportunity to address any negatives that could get in the way of an offer – or give you a heads-up that it's time to move on to other opportunities.

Brevity and Confidence

Putting together the appreciation, REV Points and enthusiastically asking for the job, the complete closing statement presented above takes about 60 seconds. It is important to keep this statement brief and not hold the interviewer hostage with a lengthy speech at this point.

It's also crucial to make this statement with body language that projects confidence and enthusiasm. In general, that's likely to mean sitting up straight, leaning in slightly and smiling, especially when you say your last words and as you shake hands before leaving.

Realize that in asking for the job you are actually *offering* something of great value: your abilities, time and dedication. You're offering your ongoing partnership and commitment. Allow yourself to rest in the dignity and power of that truth.

Whether this was a preliminary interview or the last, your next step is to follow up as strategically as you interviewed. And as with your closing statement, it's more than just a "thank you."

CHAPTER 16

Follow Up to Stand Out

Motivation will almost always beat mere talent.

– Norman Ralph Augustine

In a close race between candidates with roughly equal qualifications, often the deciding factor is the motivation and enthusiasm shown by the candidate. Maybe that's why one in five hiring managers say they would be less likely to hire a candidate who didn't send a "thank you" message.

So just sending the message puts you a step ahead. And what about doing it really *well?*

Note-taking for Smart Follow-up

Whether or not you take notes *during* your interviews, make time to do so immediately afterwards. Before you go home, while the interview is fresh in your mind, sit in your car or in a coffee shop and note the following:

- Names and roles of all the people you met

- Facts you learned about the job, the company and the industry

- Stories you told, or didn't get around to telling

- Any other topics that were discussed, whether job-related or chitchat

- Which of your qualifications and accomplishments they seemed most pleased about

- Any resistance or concerns they seemed to have

- Information about next steps in the process

These notes will be a big help in crafting intelligent, customized follow-up messages (as well as preparing for the next interview).

Beyond "Thank You"

The term "thank you letter" is a bit misleading. Even aside from demonstrating enthusiasm and good manners, your post-interview follow-up message can actually accomplish several important goals.

1. **Confirm that you're still interested.** It's very important to an employer to know whether you're still a candidate. For all the employer knows, you may have changed your mind after the interview.

2. **Show appreciation and warmth.** Say "thank you" again. Mention something you enjoyed about speaking with them, or something that impressed you

about the office. Maybe make a friendly reference to some item of chitchat. "Thanks for making time to meet with me in the middle of your rush project. I hope that's going well today."

3. **Remind them why you're the right person for the job.** Yes, you just (hopefully) made that clear in your interview yesterday, but maybe you were one of three interviewees that day and four earlier in the week, all of whom are beginning to blur together in the employer's mind. If you feel like you're repeating your message too much, find a new way to say it.

4. **If necessary, correct any omissions, misimpressions or other issues.** Did you misstate some facts out of nervousness? Did your external recruiter give you some feedback on a concern the employer expressed to her? Sometimes it can be helpful to address it in your follow-up message. But make sure you don't come across as defensive or call attention to a misstep that the interviewer may not have even noticed.

5. **Continue the conversation.** What story or qualification did you not get a chance to bring up at the time? What could you add about some industry trend or company project that was discussed at the interview? Research it. Maybe there's an interesting link you can send.

Can you accomplish all of these things in one letter? Probably not, given that it needs to be brief – no more than a few short paragraphs. You might save some of these ideas for later follow-ups.

How, Who and When?

Is it better to send an email, a formal letter or a handwritten note? Consider your industry first. In a conservative industry like finance or law, a hardcopy letter would be appropriate, or a handwritten note card could add a gracious personal touch. In IT or software, on the other hand, an email would better fit the culture.

Who should you send the follow-up to? Everyone who interviewed you, preferably as separate, personalized messages.

How soon after the interview? Very promptly, especially if a decision is expected soon. Ideally, time your first follow-up message to arrive by the next day.

Staying at Top of Mind

Interview processes can stretch out for many weeks (even months). You need to stay on the decision maker's radar screen. If you're the only candidate who keeps in touch, great — you'll be seen as the one who *really* wants the job. So it can be effective to drop the hiring manager a note or a phone call (perhaps varying your method of approach) on a regular basis until the decision is made.

Will this be viewed as "pestering"? It will if you keep asking about the decision they haven't made yet. Instead, focus on being helpful — for example, asking whether they need any further information — and continuing the conversation.

How often should you follow up? It depends on the circumstances, including the nature of the job. If you're pursuing a role as a manager, sales rep or project manager, for example, persistence and assertiveness are expected of you. If you've interviewed for a technical role, your approach can be more low-key. But don't let the decision maker forget about you.

If you feel this is too forward, you can basically ask for permission during the final interview. "May I check in with an email or phone call at some point to see if you need any other information?"

Staying Motivated When You Don't Hear Back

This part is hard. There's a lot of discussion in human resources circles these days about "the candidate experience," which in many hiring processes leaves much to be desired. But it's not the task of this book, nor is it your task as the job seeker, to fix the business world's recruiting practices.

The real practical question is, what do *you* need to do to stay motivated? If you expect to hear back after each message, your likely outcome is discouragement, self-doubt or even resentment.

The best thing you can do is remove your ego from the picture, follow up because it's smart strategy, and let go of the outcome. Paradoxically, that gives you the best chance of getting the outcome you want.

If You've Followed Up Several Times with No Reply

At a certain point it's time for a final message, in which you reiterate your interest but state that "at this point I've had to focus my attention on other opportunities." Make it clear you would still be happy to meet for another interview or a cup of coffee anytime.

If You Don't Get the Job

Believe it or not, there can be value in a final thank-you message after you've heard that you won't be hired, especially if you were one of the top candidates and/or had a strong rapport with the hiring manager. Why?

A manager you've interviewed with is an extra-valuable networking candidate, to say the least. She is well acquainted with your skills and probably thinks highly of you. And she is in a good position to recommend you to others in the company or even to hire you for some role that may open in the future – maybe even the very near future. For example, the new hire may not work out.

So one more time, thank them for their time, wish them the best of success, and indicate a general interest in keeping in touch, perhaps mentioning that you look forward to seeing them at a certain industry event in the future. If you're interested in consulting for the company, you might discuss how you could be a resource. At the very least, you can invite them to connect on LinkedIn.

As you might imagine, this level of follow-up is rare among job seekers. Once again, you will stand out as a mature, cordial individual with a serious interest in the company.

And remember, "no" doesn't mean "never." It just means "not now." If you check the company's website or LinkedIn job listings later, you may find the position is still open. Maybe they had trouble finding the right person, or they hired someone who didn't work out. It might be worth checking with human resources to see if they'd like to revisit your qualifications.

But enough about "no." Let's talk about "yes," that moment when you hear that the job is yours. It's a wonderful moment, and also a crucial one. Do you immediately accept, without discussing the compensation package or negotiating anything? Do you immediately quit your current job? And what about that other company you just interviewed with? Will you have more than one offer to juggle?

With just a bit more attention to strategy, you can ensure a smooth path into your new job.

CHAPTER 17

The Big Moment: Handling Offers

It is in your moments of decision that your
destiny is shaped.

– Tony Robbins

The moment you're offered a job can be a mini-whirlwind of excitement joy, relief, nervousness, you name it. You may be tempted to scream "YES!" – quickly, before they can change their mind!

Many a job seeker has done exactly that, only to think later, "I sure wish I had thought about … (negotiating the starting date, the salary, leaving early on Tuesdays? the potential offer from that other company?) … before I said yes."

Do yourself a favor. Have a plan for handling this important turning point in your career.

Buying Yourself Some Time to Think

When you receive the offer, chances are that one of the following will be true for you:

+ Certain aspects of the offer – maybe salary, the start date or the work schedule – could be better, and you have no reason to think the employer won't negotiate.

+ You have been interviewing elsewhere and may be close to an offer from another company.

+ You're not entirely sure this job is the right one. You have questions in your mind, such as:

    + Is this company financially stable? Any chance of layoffs in the next year or two?

    + Is this the right company culture for me?

    + Is there anything about the work schedule, the commute or the working conditions that's going to get old fast?

    + What effect would this job have on my long-term career path?

    + Can I live on this salary?

    + Will I need to relocate? Will my family and I be happy in the new place?

    + Can I afford to wait for a better opportunity?

If so, I suggest you give an answer like this:

"This is a very exciting offer! I so appreciate it! Of course, it's a very important decision, so I'd like to

give it some careful thought. How soon do you need my answer?"

If you plan to negotiate, ask for a meeting:

"Is there a time tomorrow when we could meet to discuss the details of the offer?"

Whether you agree on giving an answer by Thursday, or meeting tomorrow at 1 pm to discuss details, immediately send an email confirming what has been agreed.

Confirm, Confirm, Confirm

We've all heard that it's important to get a written offer letter (and to make sure all the details are as agreed). But that's not the only point that needs to be confirmed in writing.

Opportunities have been lost because both parties were not clear about the next steps. "We didn't hear back from you (within the timeframe we assumed you understood), so we had to move on." Whether you're asking for time to think, for an answer to a question, or for an opportunity to discuss (negotiate) details of the offer, make sure the next step is confirmed in writing.

Keep a pleasant tone about it. You're simply being thorough and professional for the benefit of all concerned.

Will You Negotiate?

Not all job offers can be negotiated. Entry-level and some public sector job offers are commonly (although not always) non-negotiable, and some corporations have a policy of not negotiating certain aspects of the job, such as salary. But most employers expect some negotiation to occur – more than 80% according to a survey by salary.com.

If you have never negotiated a job offer before, or are not sure you can, here are some reasons to consider taking the leap:

- **You'll probably end up with a better offer if you negotiate.** Salary increases of $5K are very common not to mention other perks.

- **It's not just about your initial salary.** Future raises will be based on a percentage of the salary you obtain now. The salary of future job offers will be influenced by it.

- **Assertiveness and negotiation may be on-the-job skills.** Why not demonstrate them now?

- **They may expect it and respect you more for it.** Negotiating shows that you believe in your value.

- **It is highly unlikely they will withdraw the offer.** As long as you communicate clearly, get agreements in writing, and take a positive and reasonable approach throughout the process, there is little risk. It would be highly unprofessional for an employer to withdraw an offer just because you made a reasonable effort to negotiate.

- **You're going to feel very empowered once you do it!**

What Can Be Negotiated?

Salary isn't everything. It's actually a good idea to negotiate on more than one aspect of the package. That way, if they can't meet your request in one area, they're likely to make it up to you on something else.

Salary and Benefits:
+ Base salary
+ Timing of first salary review
+ Signing bonus
+ Annual / quarterly bonuses
+ Stock options and other equity grants
+ Health benefits (type and level of benefits, effective date)
+ Retirement / termination pay (pension plans, severance packages)
+ Tuition reimbursement
+ Sick days / personal time off (PTO)
+ Vacations (amount of, or the fact that you already have something scheduled)
+ Relocation assistance, including reimbursement for house-hunting trips (with spouse or partner) before start date
+ Employee discounts
+ Company car
+ Mileage reimbursement

+ Expense account

+ Executive options such as: reimbursement of benefits lost by leaving another employer, additional pensions/insurance, nonqualified deferred compensation plans (NQDCs), supplemental executive retirement plans (SERPs), first class business travel, special parking, etc.

Other:

+ Start date

+ Hours, flexible work schedules

+ Telecommuting

+ Job title when starting

+ Higher title after a specified time period

+ Job responsibilities

Negotiating Tactics

Negotiating is an art, and many articles and books have been written offering various, sometimes conflicting approaches. It's beyond the scope of this book to add to that discussion. However, I will offer a few key points.

+ It's best to have a firm, written offer of employment before beginning to negotiate the details.

+ Do some research so you know what you're worth in the marketplace.

+ Know your walk-away point, the lowest offer you would accept.

+ Nurture good relationships throughout the process.

+ Negotiate with the same positive attitude, respect and ethics the employer wants to see on the job.

+ Look for win-win solutions, and realize that it's truly in both parties' interests to craft a package that will keep you happy.

+ Focus on interests and needs rather than hard-and-fast positions. Be open to alternative ways of addressing your interests.

+ Realize that the negotiation may not be completed in one meeting. It's a process.

Juggling Two or More Offers

Let's say you get an offer at Company #1, but you have also interviewed at Company #2 and may be close to an attractive offer there as well. What can you do?

Tell Company #2 you have a firm offer elsewhere, and ask whether they can accelerate the process.

Politely decline to state the specifics of the offer, such as salary; that information is confidential to Company #1. (You can tell them Company #1's name if it seems helpful.)

Meanwhile, negotiate for time at Company #1. Taking up to a week to accept an offer is not unusual; even longer for senior positions or if a relocation is involved. If they're in a hurry, express understanding about their situation while being assertive about what you need. It's an important decision, after all. Let them know you have another offer – or impending offer – that you need to consider, but make sure they understand you are equally (or more) interested in their offer.

When you finally choose which job to accept, inform both parties verbally and in writing. Maintain a positive relationship with Company #2. You never know what opportunities may arise there in future, or who they may talk to.

Be very skeptical of any counter-offer you might receive from your current employer. Staying in an existing job because they sweetened the deal tends to turn out badly. Your company would see you as a flight risk, so you'd probably be passed over for important projects and promotions. Your political clout would disappear and you'd essentially be a lame duck. Worse, the counter-offer might be intended only to keep you in place until they can find a replacement – at which time you'd be let go. Your other opportunities, of course, would be long gone.

Once you accept an offer, should you turn it down if a better one comes along? Generally, no. Withdrawing your acceptance is likely to cause very hard feelings. You would be breaking a promise upon which the employer will have made plans, including ceasing to pursue other candidates. They may have actually said "no" to their second-choice candidate, who may now be unavailable. If you've already started at the job the inconvenience and expense to the employer can be significant. All of this can permanently damage your reputation.

That said, there may be times when the damage could conceivably be worth it. Maybe the second job offer is an absolute dream job that will take your career to a whole new level. Or maybe the job you accepted has turned out to be very different than described, and/or there is something very wrong with it and it clearly won't work out. In either of these cases, apologize to your employer, explain the situation honestly and tactfully, and do anything in your power to help make it better.

Ending a job search, and starting a new job, is a significant turning point in life. The first thing to do is to celebrate! Woo-hoo!

The second thing to do is give a little thought to career management. Unless you're sure this is the last job you'll ever have in your life – which is rarely the case in today's world – you can do yourself a big favor by making this transition in a manner that supports your future career growth. The final, brief chapter will help you navigate this transition and launch yourself into a successful start in your new role.

CHAPTER 18

You've Got the Job! – a Moment for Career Management

Arriving at one goal is the starting point to another.

– John Dewey

From the moment you accept a new job to your first glowing performance review on the new job, career transition can be a bit of a roller coaster ride – exciting, hectic, even stressful. You get caught up in the whirlwind of that. But it's also an important moment for some conscious career management.

Managing Your Career

Career management means realizing that although your new job is at XYZ Inc., your real, lifetime employer is You Inc., and you're the leader of that enterprise.

Once upon a time we could depend on our employers for financial security. Today, there is more security to be had from a well-managed career than from any individual job. Likewise, your personal and professional fulfillment are up to you.

This advice is nothing new, but since it's part of a paradigm shift – a change in our mindset as a culture – we need to be reminded of it.

Managing "Me, Inc." through your job transition means you're in charge of:

- *Product Development* – You and your skills are the product. What do you want to learn while you're in this job?

- *Talent Development and Advancement* – Do you want to advance within the company, or beyond it? To what role(s)? How will you get there?

- *Finance* – If you've been unemployed, you may have become painfully aware that you can't count on a steady income at all times in your life. What's your plan to create or replenish your between-jobs fund?

- *Marketing Communications* – Your current campaign is ending successfully! And good career marketing is ongoing.

Speaking of marketing communications, during this job search, did you find yourself thinking "I wish I had done (X) before I needed to start looking for a new job"? Did you wish you had…

…Kept track of accomplishments and kudos on the

job, as "resume material"?

...Taken home copies of your performance reviews?

...Kept your resume and LinkedIn profile updated?

...Built a network and stayed in touch?

...Stayed on better terms with past employers?

If so, plan on taking these steps as you go along, so next time it can all be *easier* and *even more successful!*

Let's look at some specific actions that will support your career as you're leaving your old job and getting ready to start your new one.

Giving Notice and Transitioning Out

Before giving notice, make sure you have the new job offer in writing, including the start date. If you have any doubts whether that job will really be there – for example, if the company is undergoing extreme turmoil – clarify that with your boss-to-be before you give notice. New jobs have been known to vanish between the offer and the start date.

Gather resume-fodder details while you still can. Giving notice doesn't necessarily mean the company will want you to stay, and you may suddenly lose access to your computer and hardcopy files. So before giving notice, and without violating agreements or ethics, gather up information that may be helpful in your next job search, such as copies of your performance reviews and details about your accomplishments (how much you increased sales last year, etc.).

Be clear what's yours and what's theirs. Does your LinkedIn profile belong to you, even though your employer helped you set it up and it's connected to your business email address? Do you own your customer contacts or not? Disputes have arisen over these types of information.

Give notice verbally and in writing. Break the news to your supervisor first, in a private meeting, and agree on how and when the announcement will be made to others. Then write an email or letter stating briefly that you are resigning and when your last day will be. Stating why you are leaving is not necessary, but do include appreciation and thanks, even – or especially! – if the vibes are not gloriously warm.

How much notice should you give? Two weeks' notice is standard; offering less is generally considered unprofessional. You might even want to offer more if leaving in two weeks would cause a hardship for the team. But don't let it drag on and on. Your future is with the new company, so put that relationship first. Also consider your own needs for rest and recuperation. You may need to negotiate with both employers to get some time off in between. *Enjoy some time off if you possibly can!* Starting a new job takes a lot of energy.

Go out on a positive note. Past employers and co-workers are VIPs in your career network for many reasons – as sources of references, recommendations and information; for their influence on your reputation; and hopefully even as friends. So treat them well. Be willing to train your replacement. Create documentation for the next person in the role. Share all those tips nobody knows better than you.

Replacing Job Search with Ongoing Career Communications

Continue and nurture relationships with the people you've met in your search. Share your good news with everyone who helped you in any way. Maybe treat somebody to a meal to celebrate together and show appreciation for their support. Don't be one of those people who only get in touch when they want something.

Update and improve your LinkedIn profile now; this is the very best time to do it. A year or two from now you may be looking at new opportunities, but spiffing up your profile at that point may arouse suspicion. Doing it now is safer, and will also help you look good to new colleagues who may be curious about you. Ask for recommendations from people at the job you're leaving, especially your former boss. (Aren't you glad you were nice on your way out?) Add your new job, either right before you start or, if you have any doubts about whether it will work out, after you've been on the job a little while. Don't put it off too long.

File away notes for your next job search. If you've created various versions of your resume, gathered a lot of useful information about companies and job titles, and so on, you may want to refer to these items at some point in the future. Put them where you'll be able to find them.

On Your New Job

If you've read this book, I'm guessing you work hard – and strategically – for what you want, and that you're also smart about seeking out new knowledge and outside expertise to support your efforts. These qualities will serve you well in your new workplace.

Your first days and months on the job will be about forming relationships, learning, and making a point of achieving early wins to quickly establish yourself as a valuable team member. All of that is beyond the scope of this book, but much has been written by others about making a great first impression at your new job and ensuring that the crucial first few months will be evaluated positively.

May your new job and your career be a rich source of everything you want from it, whether that be exciting challenges and growth, making a difference, prosperity, security, camaraderie or appreciation. I wish you "all of the above"!

You only live once, but if you do it right, once is enough.

– Mae West

About the Author and Interview Coaching

Thea Kelley provides personalized, one-on-one interview coaching and related career services to help you get a great job, sooner.

Drawing upon 20+ years of coaching, career services, writing and editing experience, she serves individuals nationwide and across all occupations and industries. Thea's clients have successfully landed roles from entry level to senior executive, often surmounting major obstacles to do so. She can help you identify your unique value to employers and tell your story credibly and flawlessly.

Thea has been interviewed about interview preparation and salary negotiation on VoiceAmerica Online Talk Radio. She has contributed to two multi-author books, *Find Your Fit: A Practical Guide to Landing a Job You'll Love* and *Modernize Your Resume*.

A Certified Employment Interview Consultant, Certified Professional Resume Writer, and Online Professional Networking Strategist, Thea stays current through membership in professional groups including Career Thought Leaders, Career Directors International and the Professional Association of Resume Writers and Career Coaches.

Her office is located in Albany, California (just north of Berkeley) in the San Francisco Bay Area.

Email Thea at **thea@theakelley.com**
Visit her website at **www.theakelley.com**
Subscribe to her blog at **www.theakelley.com/blog**

Acknowledgments

It's an honor to help people achieve their career goals, and I'm grateful for all I've learned from my clients and students over the years.

I'm also deeply appreciative to my friend and colleague Irene Marshall for her generous attention and wise comments on the draft, and to my discerning husband Eric Kampman, without whom this book would contain way! too! many! exclamation points!

Last but certainly not least, I appreciate you who are reading this book. Please let me know what you think.

General Index

Index of Interview Questions